# The Work Environment

# LAW AT WORK

# The Work Environment

The law of health, safety and welfare

**Second edition**

# Patricia Leighton

NICHOLAS BREALEY
PUBLISHING

LONDON

This second edition first published in Great Britain by
Nicholas Brealey Publishing Limited in 1997

36 John Street
London
WC1N 2AT, UK
Tel: +44 (0)171 430 0224
*Fax: +44 (0)171 404 8311*

17470 Sonoma Highway
Sonoma
California 95476, USA
Tel: (707) 939 7570
*Fax: (707) 938 3515*

http://nbrealey-books.com

First edition published in 1991

ISBN 1-85788-104-4

**British Library Cataloguing in Publication Data**
A catalogue record for this book is available from the British Library.

Printed in Finland by Werner Söderström Oy.

# Contents

# Major Statutes and Regulations

Chemicals (Hazard Information and Packaging for Supply) Regulations 1994

Construction (Design and Management) Regulations 1994

Construction (Health, Safety and Welfare) Regulations 1996

Control of Asbestos at Work Regulations 1987

Control of Substances Hazardous to Health Regulations 1988 (COSHH)

Consumer Protection Act 1987

Deregulation and Contracting Out Act 1994

Electricity at Work Regulations 1989

Employer's Liability (Compulsory Insurance) Act 1969

Employment Rights Act 1996

Enforcement Authority Regulations 1989

Environment Protection Act 1990

Factories Act 1961

Fire Safety and Safety of Places of Sport Act 1987

Health and Safety at Work Act 1974 (HSWA)

Health and Safety (Information for Employees) Regulations 1989

Health and Safety (Consultation with Employees) Regulations 1996

Health and Safety (Young Persons) Regulations 1996

Health and Safety (Safety Signs and Signals) Regulations 1996

Highly Flammable Liquids and Liquified Petroleum Gases Regulations 1972

Ionising Radiation Regulations 1958

Iron and Steel Foundries Regulations 1953

Management of Health and Safety at Work Regulations, 1992 (MOHSWR)

Manual Handling Regulations 1992

Misuse of Drugs Act 1971

Noise at Work Regulations 1989

Occupiers' Liability Act 1957 (OLA)

Offices, Shops and Railway Premises Act 1963

Reporting of Injuries, Diseases and Dangerous Occurrences Regulations 1985 (RIDDOR); 1995, 1996

Safety Representatives and Safety Committees Regulations 1977

Use of Work Equipment Regulations 1992

Workplace Health, Safety and Welfare Regulations 1992

Working Time Directive 1993

# *Cases*

# *Abbreviations*

---

ACOP — Approved Code of Practice

BSD — Breach of statutory duty

COSHH — Control of Substances Hazardous to Health Regulations 1988

DSE — Display screen equipment

EU — European Union

FA — Factories Act 1961

ILO — International Labour Office

HSE — Health and Safety Executive

HSWA — Health and Safety at Work Act 1974

MHSWR — Management of Health and Safety at Work Regulations 1992

MEL — Maximum exposure levels

OLA — Occupiers' Liability Act 1957

PPE — Personal protective equipment

RIDDOR — Reporting of Injuries, Diseases and Dangerous Occurrences Regulations 1985/1995

RoSPA — Royal Society for the Prevention of Accidents

VDU — Visual Display Unit

# 1

# *Why Take Health and Safety Law Seriously?*

From a situation only a decade ago when health and safety was generally perceived as worthy, technical and maybe boring, it has now reached centre stage and is widely debated. It is vitally important that anyone aiming to understand and comply with health and safety law has a clear view of the objectives of law, i.e. how law aims to reduce the incidence of accidents and ill health at work. Detail is important but the basic strategy of law must also be understood.

Until quite recently, many employment texts ignored the topic of health and safety at work or relegated it to a backwater. The Health and Safety at Work Act 1974 appeared to deal effectively with most of the issues surrounding accidents at work. It promoted the idea of employer and employees sharing responsibility for a safe workplace and gave the trade unions a key role. The Act retained criminal law sanctions for breaches of law, but increased the powers of the safety inspectorates to prevent harm through their use of Improvement and Prohibition

Notices. These were seen as simple and speedy enforcement procedures.

The problem is that, despite people in the UK tending to work in less dangerous occupations, the use of information technology and the growth of service industries, accident and ill-health rates have remained stubbornly high. It is not difficult to identify some of the reasons for this. Clearly, there have been economic pressures to retain competitiveness. There have also been moves towards adopting the so-called flexible workforce. This may make sense for the employer in economic terms, but health and safety research indicates that flexible/atypical workers, such as those on temporary contracts, are more prone to injuries and accidents than are 'standard' workers. Employing a flexible workforce puts considerable demands on management and information systems, which are central to effective compliance with health and safety laws.

Along with high accident and ill-health records, the second major reason to take the law seriously is that there is far more of it, it is being rigorously enforced and it is affecting a far wider range of work issues and problems. Law is no longer geared to apparently dangerous and heavy industries but has equal relevance to *all* workplaces.

It is also important to note the major changes in the nature and approach of this law which have been generated by the European health and safety agenda. In essence, health and safety law is established through international standards and many ideas for new laws and new approaches come from outside the UK. Law builds on best practice, is informed by research and aims to establish clear guidelines for employers. It identifies 'problem' industries, activities and processes and develops an appropriate response.

There has been talk recently of deregulating health and safety law. It is, indeed, likely that the process of removing out-of-date, complex or irrelevant laws from the statute book will continue. However, due to its membership of the European Union, the UK is obliged to comply with European legislation and there is, in reality, little scope for weakening or avoiding legislative demands.

## OTHER URGENT REASONS

- The last few years have seen a series of major disasters involving members of the public as well as employees, causing massive loss of life: Zeebrugge, the King's Cross fire, Piper Alpha, the *Marchioness*, the *Estonia* and the Lyme Bay canoeing accident. Public inquiries and commentators have stressed the need for more effective management and adequate resources to ensure health and safety. Disasters such as these have considerably heightened public awareness and concern.

• In 1995 there was the first successful manslaughter prosecution for a work-related accident; there are proposals for a 'new' offence of corporate manslaughter which will have particular relevance for major accidents and disasters.

• The costs of accidents and ill-health at work are now well documented, including insurance costs. The UK has one of the highest employee absence rates in Europe. Research studies show that accidents can have major impacts on running costs, profitability and productivity. The HSE report *The Costs of Accidents at Work* (1993) heightened awareness of the often hidden and uninsured losses caused by accidents. Figure 1.1 illustrates this; it also suggests that a similar analysis can be applied to illness.

   The 'icebergs' are used to illustrate the fact that employers can insure against *some* losses but, for every £1 of loss which an insurance policy covers, far higher losses will be caused for which there is, typically, no insurance protection.

• In 1993 the first successful claim was made for illness caused by passive smoking; in 1994 the first successful claim was brought for work-related stress. Health issues as well as accidents are increasingly recognised by law. This includes musculo-skeletal disorders such as tenosynovitis, more popularly referred to as repetitive strain injury (RSI). Levels of compensation in this area have grown rapidly.

• Accident rates continue to be high. The Health and Safety Executive (HSE) recognises that only around a third of all reportable accidents are actually reported. There are also certain industries and activities which generate high accident statistics – construction, transport and extractive industries, for example.

## THE NEW AGENDA

A wider range of workplace and work-related problems are now key elements of health and safety law. Included here are:

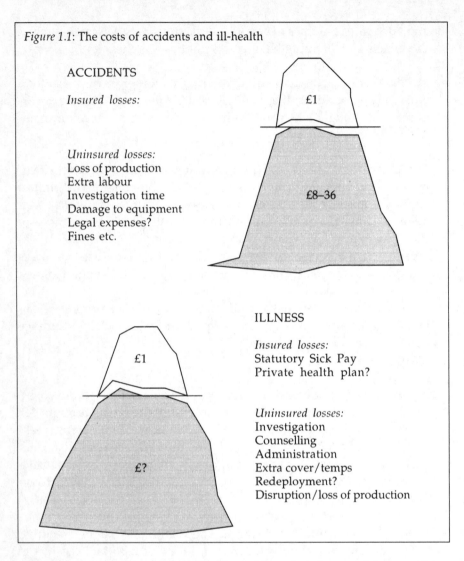

Figure 1.1: The costs of accidents and ill-health

ACCIDENTS

Insured losses:

Uninsured losses:
Loss of production
Extra labour
Investigation time
Damage to equipment
Legal expenses?
Fines etc.

£1

£8–36

£1

£?

ILLNESS

Insured losses:
Statutory Sick Pay
Private health plan?

Uninsured losses:
Investigation
Counselling
Administration
Extra cover/temps
Redeployment?
Disruption/loss of production

- violence or threats of violence from fellow workers and/or members of the public;

- drug and alcohol abuse;

- harassment and bullying;

- excess working hours; stress and fatigue;

- 'sick building syndrome' and similar phenomena.

These developments have marked a clear shift away from traditional health and safety law. This was devised for industry, usually male-dominated workplaces seen as dangerous. Today, law not only recognises these wider concerns but applies a consistent and coherent approach, regardless of occupation, sector or type of workplace.

## WHAT DOES THIS BOOK COVER?

The law of the work environment is both varied and complex. Each area of law operates to achieve different objectives, uses different legal procedures and operates in a different context. This book aims to be up to date, accessible and to provide guidance on law and its application in order to enable organisations and managers to establish appropriate policies, structures and practices. The main areas of law covered are outlined in Table 1.1.

---

*Table 1.1*: Major areas of health and safety law

| Law | Role of law/outcome |
| --- | --- |
| HSWA 1974/MHSW Regulations 1992 legislation | Prosecution Improvement/Prohibition Notices |
| Specific safety legislation | Prosecution Improvement/Prohibition Notices |
| Law of negligence | Compensation where defendant has failed to show reasonable care |
| Breach of statutory duty (injuries) | Compensation where breach of duty causes harm |
| Contract of employment | Compensation where breach of |

---

The main focus of the book is on the Health and Safety at Work Act 1974 (HSWA), which sets out the general statutory framework but was substantially refined by the Management of Health and Safety at Work Regulations 1992 (MHSWR) and supporting regulations. Legislation deals with safety policies, equipment, working practices, information, training and supervision, as well as premises and the handling, storage and transportation of substances. Duties are imposed on employers, employees and the self-employed, and on those whose premises are used by others or who supply equipment in connection with work. Most importantly, management responsibility for health and safety will be explored in detail.

The book also considers some specific areas of statutory regulation, for example the Control of Substances Hazardous to Health Regulations 1988 (COSHH), Manual Handling Regulations 1992, the rules applicable to women when pregnant and the regulation of working time.

However, regulation also arises through other areas of law, many of which have become more important during the last few years. The law of negligence relating to both work activities and the state of premises has always had a vital role to play in providing compensation for those injured or suffering ill-health at work, as have various statutes which, if broken, can sometimes also entitle victims to compensation.

The contract of employment applies in that it requires employers not only to provide a safe workplace, but to support employees affected by the quality of the work environment. Many unfair dismissal claims taken to industrial tribunals turn on the alleged demands of an employer which exposed employees to major risks. Sometimes employers are accused of being grossly insensitive to employees' anxieties about, for example, smoking, harassment or violence at work.

Other areas of law, such as the law of nuisance and product liability, affect aspects of the workplace.

In order to illustrate how employing organisations have responded to legal demands, a number of case studies will be drawn on.

## How law works

It is quite feasible for a single accident or incident at a workplace to give rise to several legal outcomes. For example, an employee injured while using a newly purchased piece of equipment may be able to sue both the employer and the supplier of equipment in negligence; there may be a breach of the employee's contract of employment and the safety inspectorate may prosecute the employer and perhaps a line manager for breaches of the Health and Safety at Work Act 1974. The safety inspectorate may also close the factory or a part of it until it is safe, or order the employer to improve work conditions. In addition, the supplier may have broken product liability legislation. The situation is summarised in Figure 1.2.

It is very important to appreciate that the various areas of law have

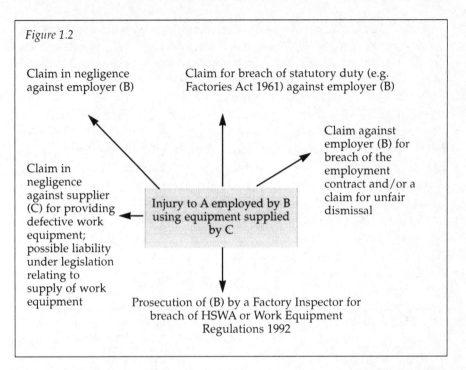

*Figure 1.2*

Claim in negligence against employer (B)

Claim for breach of statutory duty (e.g. Factories Act 1961) against employer (B)

Claim in negligence against supplier (C) for providing defective work equipment; possible liability under legislation relating to supply of work equipment

Injury to A employed by B using equipment supplied by C

Claim against employer (B) for breach of the employment contract and/or a claim for unfair dismissal

Prosecution of (B) by a Factory Inspector for breach of HSWA or Work Equipment Regulations 1992

different approaches and rules. An employer's responsibilities under HSWA generally depend on its failure to take such steps as are **'reasonably practicable'** to prevent injury to an employee. In turn, what is 'reasonably practicable' depends on what the law considers to be the checks, supervision and procedures which the reasonably well-informed employer would have carried out. This 'state-of-the-art' approach requires the particular employer to establish and maintain safety standards at the workplace equivalent to those generally applying in the industry. This will be discussed more fully in Chapters 2, 3 and 4.

However, in other areas of law, especially those dealing with hazardous activities and modern regulations derived from European law, even the achievement of general standards will not be adequate – it is essential to show that virtually every measure was taken to prevent harm. This is the concept of **'strict liability'**. In these cases, only the intervention of an act of God or *force majeure* such as freak storms or floods will allow the employer to escape liability. This standard is gradually replacing that of 'reasonable practicability'.

Therefore, an understanding of the responsibility of employers, managers and self-employed persons requires an appreciation of the legal standard expected as much as the content of the legal rule itself.

New issues which emerge in the workplace have to be accommodated in some way within the existing legal framework. Typical of these are the issues surrounding the impact of Acquired Immuno Deficiency Syndrome (AIDS); the need for organisations to restrict the times and places where smoking is permitted; the different issues which arise through employing increasing numbers of women, some of whom may be pregnant; the mounting incidence of violence at the workplace, from fellow employees but more importantly from clients/customers/members of the public generally; and stress-related disorders. In addition, the increasing awareness of certain substances – asbestos, lead and radioactive materials – and their impact on the health of employees and others has not only received wide media coverage but has given rise to legal test cases.

---

### EXAMPLES OF RECENT TEST CASES

- In November 1994 a senior social worker established that his employers – Northumberland County Council – had negligently caused him to suffer stress. The particular act of negligence had been that the employer, being aware that Mr Walker had had a nervous breakdown because of an excessive workload, had put him back in a work situation which was just as difficult when he returned from sick leave (*Walker v Northumberland CC (1994)*).

- Two ex-employees of Stockport Borough Council successfully argued that failing to deal with the effects of passive smoking was negligent. This raised the issue of the legal rights of the non-smoker, as well as the smoker. *Bland v Stockport C (1992)* and *Ferguson v Stockport C (1995)* tested non-smokers' rights. Illnesses associated with passive smoking have now been accepted as industrial accidents in a test case against the Department of Social Security.

- A keyboard worker obtained compensation from her employer in negligence for RSI because of its failure to ensure breaks and adequate seating (*McSherry v British Telecom (1993)*).

- A long-standing female employee was allegedly sexually assaulted by two managers shortly after work (*Bracebridge v Darby (1990)*). The employer inadequately investigated the complaint by the employee. This was held to be dismissal by the employer due to breach of the implied contractual obligation to investigate seriously incidents of this nature and provide a safe environment.

## THE 'EUROPEANISING' OF HEALTH AND SAFETY LAW

In the early 1990s there was an enormous output of new legislation on health and safety from the European Commission. Article 118A of the Treaty of Rome emphasises the need to improve working conditions. Proposals under this Article are passed (adopted) by the Council of Ministers by a qualified majority vote, i.e. it is not possible for one or two member states to block proposals by vetoing them. Law has developed quickly.

There are also European Commission Action Programmes on Safety, Hygiene and Health Protection, regularly updated. The European agenda is wide. Included are protection for pregnant women and regulation of hours of work and holidays. Certain types of employees also need specific health and safety protection, such as temporary employees and agency staff, those in the construction industry and on board vessels.

It is also vital to note that the future emphasis regarding health and safety measures will be on research, standardisation, monitoring and review of the effectiveness of health and safety legislation. A new Health and Safety Agency has been established in Bilbao, Spain.

Six major health and safety directives had been adopted by 1990, covering key aspects of occupational health as well as safety issues and, most importantly, dealing with structures and procedures to establish and monitor safe systems as well as safety management more generally. Other specialised areas such as carcinogens and biological agents are the subject of other measures and are now part of UK law. In addition, a range of directives have been developed on specific industries, for example construction and agriculture. The amount of activity in Europe, the level of involvement by the Health and Safety Executive and the speed of progress on proposals are significant.

It is vital to take note of European legislation, because the concepts and approach of 'Euro laws' are significantly different from those traditional in the UK. Managers with responsibility for health and safety matters at the workplace will not only have to comply with demanding legislation, but also appreciate that its priorities, approaches and legal demands are significantly different from traditional UK law. In particular, law requires managers to be proactive, to assess all workplace risks and to establish effective systems not only to achieve the appropriate safety or health standards but to ensure regular monitoring and review.

## What are the Law's Objectives?

1. To ensure that law is developed and applied so as to reduce risks at work, ideally to zero.

2. To ensure that those most at risk receive particular and appropriate protection.

3. To see improvement in standards as a core management task.

4. To ensure even standards across the EU and across all sectors, size and locations of employment.

It is also important to note that the occupational health and safety legal framework has much in common with legislation applying to the environment in general. Common approaches and common standards have been established.

## Health and Safety – What are the Facts?

For an understanding of policy directions and as a necessary context to legal regulation, it is useful to glance at the statistics on fatal and other major injuries at the workplace.

### Industry Statistics

Injury (as opposed to ill-health) figures are dominated by certain industries:

- oil/gas extraction
- mineral extraction
- metal manufacturing
- construction
- timber and wood furniture manufacturing
- rubber and plastics processing

It is also generally important to note that several other not apparently dangerous industries have growing fatal accident rates:

| Area | Fatal accidents involving employees 1993–94 | 1995–96 |
|---|:---:|:---:|
| Agriculture | 16 | 19 |
| Coal extraction | 16 | 16 |
| Transport | 28 | 21 |
| Public administration | 7 | 10 |
| Recreational and cultural services | 4 | 7 |

There has been an increase in some non-fatal types of injury:

| Type of injury | Injuries per 100,000 employees 1989–90 | 1995–96 |
|---|:---:|:---:|
| Trip or fall | 146 | 157 |
| Struck by moving vehicle | 57 | 62 |
| Exposure to harmful substance | 14 | 24 |

At the same time there has been an apparent decline in the incidence of amputation, eye damage, fire injuries and fractures.

## How many die per year?

Overall, on average, around 500 people die per year as a result of a work-related accident. Over 3000 die as a result of work-related ill-health such as asbestosis. These figures generally compare well with other parts of the EU, but as regards non-fatal accidents it should be borne in mind that not all reportable accidents are actually reported and other countries often include a wider range of accidents in their statistics, such as accidents to and from work.

Excluded from the statistics are:

- accidents to armed forces;
- road accidents to and from work;
- fatal injuries to the self-employed outside specified situations;
- railway accidents to passengers (suicides included from 1995–96).

Virtually all of these lead to significant deaths or injuries each year.

To get a good understanding of data and trends in occupational health and safety, the Annual Reports of the Health and Safety Commission (HSC), usually published in November each year, are well worth reading.

## Occupational health statistics

Statistics provide a guide to the incidence of specified occupational diseases, such as decompression sickness, vibration white finger, pneumoconiosis and asbestosis. Broadly, the level of disease is reducing, although some diseases, especially cancers, are increasing dramatically. The statistics probably suffer from under-reporting and do not yet record occupation-related disorders such as stress, backaches, headaches and many skin conditions frequently associated with work circumstances. They also do not record the impact of passive smoking at the workplace, although data on its harmful effects is beginning to emerge. RIDDOR 1996 has updated and clarified illness-reporting requirements (see Chapter 3).

## How likely are organisations to be prosecuted?

The Health and Safety at Work Act 1974 and other legislation are directly enforced in two ways:

- criminal law prosecution initiated by the safety inspectorates;

- use of enforcement notices – improvement or prohibition – served by the relevant inspectorate.

The incidence and level of fines on organisations and/or individuals where guilt has been established have steadily risen over the last few years. The average fine is now well over £3000.

It should also be noted that other areas of criminal law have relevance, including assault and manslaughter. In these situations named individuals are prosecuted, typically senior managers. In 1995 a Law Commission report called for a new offence of corporate manslaughter, which could be used where there has been management failure resulting in death.

There are, therefore, a wide range of interventions by law and managerial responsibility is increasingly being targeted. It should always be borne in mind that, although fines may not be high relative to company profits or budgets, the attendant publicity could severely damage business reputation and individual careers. The rest of this book aims to provide sufficient information for managers to be able to take a comprehensive and responsible attitude to health and safety at work.

# 2

# *The Statutory Framework for Health and Safety*

Statutes on health and safety have a long history. The first initiatives date from 1802 and 1833, and laws providing inspectors with wide powers to enter premises developed on a coherent basis from 1848. Modern legislation dates from the Factories Act 1937, the forerunner of the Factories Act 1961.

Until recently a key feature of safety legislation in the UK was its tendency to be occupation/industry specific (e.g. the Mines and Quarries Act, the Offices, Shops and Railway Premises Act) and to provide detailed regulation of the hazards peculiar to different types of workplaces. At the same time some areas of work, such as community and leisure activities, have been subject to relatively little regulation as they are outside the traditionally more dangerous occupations.

However, a milestone was reached with the Report of the Robens Committee on health and safety law in 1973. This called for a more comprehensive system of legal regulation, a clear statement of general principles and, most importantly, for law which would reflect the shared responsibility for ensuring safe work standards between employer, employee and the self-employed. The report also drew attention to the duties which employers owe to the wider public.

The report was adopted virtually in its entirety and emerged as the Health and Safety at Work Act 1974. Essentially, the Act set out the broad duties of all at work, and established a framework for safety management and safety enforcement. It did not repeal occupation- or sector-specific statutes or regulations and, although many have been amended or repealed during the period since 1974, several key statutes remain in force.

A major purpose of the legislation was to increase awareness of health and safety issues and to encourage high levels of participation by employees. It was hoped that this concept of shared responsibility would help to reduce accidents and would lead to a largely self-regulating system. This aim has not been fulfilled, although the 1974 Act provides a clearly drafted system of safety administration and policy development.

## WHAT IS THE CURRENT FRAMEWORK?

Today the statutory framework is different and more complex. There has been virtually no 'home-grown' legislation since 1989. Recent UK health and safety legislation is drawn from European Directives, in particular the Framework Directive of 1989. This established the basic legal principles and defined the legal duties of all at work. It was transposed into UK law as the Management of Health and Safety at Work Regulations 1992, which became operative in January 1993. It generally imposes duties strictly, i.e. the words 'reasonableness' or 'reasonable practicability' occur only rarely.

The key legal duties on the employer regarding health and safety (which are considered more fully in Chapter 3) are to:

- plan
- organise
- control          } health and safety at individual workplaces
- monitor
- review

These duties arise regardless of employment sector, organisation size, resources or policies. These duties are the **'irreducible minimum'** and apply to *all* work-related issues, from machinery and premises through to violence, stress and muskulo-skeletal disorders such as RSI.

The key tasks for the employer are that of risk assessment (of *all* potential health risks) and then setting up preventive measures, ideally to eliminate the risk, or at least to minimise it. For example, a particular workplace may suffer from heat and dust caused by the nature of materials being worked on. The risks include respiratory problems, along with fatigue and dehydration. The law requires the employer to assess the level of risk and identify those at risk and then to respond appropriately. This demands exploration of options – change the machines, install effective dust-extraction equipment, improve ventilation, install air conditioning, ensure workers have adequate breaks and perhaps, as a last resort, provide masks for workers.

The legal demands are clear and require effective management systems. Furthermore, law requires 'transparency', i.e. that a hypothetical safety inspector has evidence of what steps the employer was taking to respond to assessed risks.

The Management Regulations also single out specific work situations which create special risks. Included here are likely risks when employers and others share premises; when self-employed, agency or sub-contracted staff are used, with attendant problems of poor communications and inconsistent standards; and when pregnant women are involved in work which creates particular risks for them.

## WHAT OF EMPLOYEES AND THE SELF-EMPLOYED?

The Management Regulations also establish duties for employees and self-employed workers. In both cases they must comply with safety rules and procedures and notify employers if there are defects in safety standards.

These Regulations (and indeed all modern health and safety legislation) adopt a strategy which makes all people at work directly and personally responsible. They are the eyes and ears of the organisation as well as being required to comply with health and safety rules and procedures.

## WHAT ARE THE MAIN REGULATIONS?

In chronological order, these are as follows:

- Factories Act 1961
- Offices, Shops and Railway Premises Act 1963
- The Health and Safety at Work Act 1974 (HSWA)

- Safety Representatives and Safety Committees Regulations 1977
- The Reporting of Injuries, Diseases and Dangerous Occurrences Regulations 1985 (RIDDOR) (as amended 1995)
- The Control of Substances Hazardous to Health Regulations 1988 (COSHH) (amended several times since 1988)
- The Health and Safety Information for Employees Regulations 1989
- The Fire Safety and Safety of Places of Sport Act 1987
- Electricity at Work Regulations 1989
- Noise at Work Regulations 1989
- Management of Health and Safety at Work Regulations 1992 (MHSWR)*
- Workplace (Health, Safety and Welfare) Regulations 1992*
- Health and Safety (Display Screen Equipment) Regulations 1992*
- Provision and Use of Work Equipment Regulations 1992*
- Personal Protection Equipment at Work Regulations 1992*
- Manual Handling Operations Regulations 1992*
- Construction (Design and Management) Regulations 1994
- RIDDOR 1995
- Health and Safety (Consultation with Employees) Regulations 1996

* Collectively these regulations, which came into force on 1 January 1993, are popularly referred to as the 'Six Pack'.

The 1974 Act established the basic administrative framework for health and safety. It deals with institutions and procedures for the development and review of law, its enforcement and some basic health and safety structures at workplaces. The 1992 Management Regulations established the specific legal duties of all at work and management procedures which must be in place. They are concerned with safety standards at individual workplaces and the role and responsibilities of people there.

## Approved Codes of Practice (ACOP)

The Health and Safety Executive publishes considerable numbers of ACOPs and Guidance Notes. Examples are:

- Approved Code of Practice Health and Safety (First Aid) Regulations 1987
- Approved Code of Practice Control of Carcinogenic Substances 1988
- Approved Code of Practice Control of Substances Hazardous to Health 1988

Note that most of the 'Six Pack' have ACOPs.

Guidance Notes are self-evident; they suggest ways in which employers can comply with legal duties and often offer checklists and the like. Approved Codes of Practice interpret an Act or Regulations and spell out in detail the implications of the law. However, complying with a Code, or following the suggestions in a Guidance Note, is not fail-safe. The law takes the view that if Codes of Practice are followed, this is good evidence that an employer is carrying out statutory duties; but there is still a need, for example, for an employer to check for unusual developments or new hazards (see the case of the exploding boiler below).

---

### EXAMPLE – THE EXPLODING BOILER

There was an explosion in a West Midlands factory caused by a badly corroded safety valve which failed to prevent excess pressure in a steam boiler. The boiler hurtled nearly a quarter of a mile, crashed through the roof of a private house and miraculously caused only shock and abrasions to a mother and her children who were in the house at the time.

Evidence showed that the faulty valve had led to a build-up of pressure of ten times the norm. The company was prosecuted under section 33 (7) of the Factories Act 1961, but argued that it could not be guilty as it had complied with statutory demands for internal examination of the boiler every 11 months and had also inspected it externally every three months.

The view of the Magistrates' Court was that the corrosion was so severe that there was inadequate maintenance; the fact that the company had complied with statutory rules and had apparently gone beyond recommended procedures was inadequate. It was no substitute for 'constant vigilance', especially with such dangerous equipment. *(R v Fields Wholesale Meats*, 1987)

---

## WHAT STANDARD DOES THE LAW EXPECT?

This is one of the most difficult legal questions. Does the law expect you to do everything, whatever the cost or difficulty of eradicating risks? Is it adequate if you do your best? Or all you can afford? What if you were unaware of the law or a new law? Or you had had no accidents in the past and felt it was appropriate to conclude that the workplace was 'safe'?

It can be firmly stated that ignorance of the law or a failure to understand it is never a defence. It is also important to read the law itself and

## Two examples

### The collapsing roof

An employee in a gypsum mine was injured through a collapse attributed to a rare geological fault called slickenside.

The allegation was that the mining company had failed to make the mine roof safe 'so far as was reasonably practicable'. It was decided that the mining company was not in breach of mining safety legislation. The court drew attention to the following circumstances:

- the rarity of the incident (no previous one in 20 years);

- the cause of the collapse was natural, not manmade;

- latent defects in the mine roof would not have been detected by superficial/visual examination;

- providing an expensive systematic roof support would not necessarily have prevented the fall, although it might have lessened its impact.

(*Adnett v K and L Steel Founders and Engineers Ltd*, 1953)

### The vulnerable building society staff

An inspector alleged that a building society was not taking 'reasonably practicable' steps under HSWA to protect counter staff from thieves entering the building. They should have erected protective screens ('bandit' screens).

The court decided that the risk of attack was relatively slight, that staff had been trained not to resist thieves and that screens would counteract the desired image of the society towards 'friendly informality and confidence building in would-be customers'. There was no breach of law. Today, the decision might well be different in the light of a massive increase in attacks. (*West Bromwich Building Society v Townsend*, 1983)

not guess what it means or rely on popular opinion. Law can never be ignored and it is not 'negotiable'.

In setting standards, law is mindful of two important principles. First, that of **proportionality**, i.e. that the law should not require measures which are totally excessive, bearing in mind the low level of a particular risk. The chance that a building might be flooded is real, but in most situations very remote. Law would not require all employees to be provided with sub-aqua equipment, life rafts or safety flares! However, this principle should not be confused with a tolerance of accidents or an acceptance that they cannot be prevented. Most accidents have a human trail, i.e. human error has caused or contributed to them. There is also no correlation between a minor error and a minor accident – minor errors can have disastrous consequences. Most accidents are preceded by warning signs (a 'near miss' etc.) and subsequently commentators make statements such as: 'It was an accident waiting to happen.' Law requires appropriate measures, vigilance and a proper response to near misses and incidents.

The second principle is **enforceability**, i.e. that the law should be capable of being effectively enforced. This means that breaches of law should be able to be detected and those apparently guilty successfully prosecuted. Law is discredited if prosecutions are rare and/or fail. All this is easier if clear demands on employers are established through well-drafted laws and those affected by law understand and support the standards.

It has always to be kept in mind that at the end of the day the role of law itself is to prevent accidents and ill-health by using sensible and well-understood strategies.

So what is the standard? Traditionally in UK law it has been 'so far as is reasonably practicable'.

People are not required to eliminate every risk in every situation. There is, rather, a need to make a reasonable assessment of risk and to provide a reasonable response, including its costs and likelihood of preventing harm.

## WHAT IF THERE IS WILFUL MISCONDUCT?

'Practicable' steps can require employers to anticipate and provide for lapses of concentration or, in extreme cases, criminal conduct by others. The employer should provide a structured and well-supervised environment. However, law has not always made the employer liable, as shown by the recent example given on the next page.

A word of caution has to be entered about this decision. First, the accident predates the COSHH Regulations 1988 which may have laid down more rigorous expectations of both the client and subcontractor; and second, it is likely that in the 1990s, especially with pressure for higher standards, new demands from Europe and recent regulations, more attention might have been paid to the lack of awareness and response by the client to the working methods of the subcontractor.

The phrase 'reasonable practicability' is flexible, but it is hard to enforce. Its application depends on the nature of work, the degree of risk, the scope of risk and the effort and cost of minimising or eliminating risk. As one judge put it in the leading case on the meaning of the phrase, 'if the measures necessary for averting the risk (whether in terms of money, time or trouble) are assessed and the risk is "disproportionately insignificant" in relation to the sacrifice an employer will

EXAMPLE – THE PAINT SHOP FIRE

At a large car manufacturers, plant cleaning of the paint shop was carried out by subcontractors. The agreed work procedures between the manufacturer and the subcontractor included the rule that a sump should not be cleaned while a paint booth above it was occupied. This rule was disregarded with the effect that employees of the subcontractor were working in both places when a flash fire erupted in the sump, killing the employee working there.

The car manufacturer was prosecuted for breach of s4(2) HSWA for failing to take measures 'as far as reasonably practicable' so that its premises, plant and substances were safe and without risks to health when being used for work by persons other than their own employees. Specifically, the argument was that the equipment was potentially unsafe and the ventilation inadequate.

It was decided by the House of Lords that the manufacturer had not broken the law. Although the premises were indeed unsafe, the evidence was that there was a series of factors leading up to the fatal accident, including interference with the equipment by the employees, all of which were contrary to instructions. The manufacturers could not be reasonably expected to take measures to make their premises safe 'against unanticipated misuse'. (*Mailer v Austin Rover Group*, 1988)

have no need to take further steps' (Edwards v National Coal Board, 1949).

Although the standard is still used in some recent regulations, it has been generally supplanted by the clearer and probably more demanding standard largely derived from European law. This is the standard of 'strict liability'.

A RECENT APPLICATION OF THE LEGAL STANDARD – THE EXPLODING LAMP

Octel employed subcontractors to clean storage tanks. The contractors had been used regularly in the past and were familiar with the demands of the task. The contractors' workman borrowed a lamp from the client, Octel. The lamp was inappropriate as it did not meet safety standards required when working in an enclosed space and using chemicals. The workman dropped the lamp, there was an explosion and fire and he was killed.

Octel was prosecuted for failure of care to a third party – the workman. The prosecution was successful. The company had failed to take reasonably practicable steps to protect him and had provided defective equipment. (*R v Octel*, 1996)

## WHAT IS STRICT LIABILITY?

Many health and safety statutes, especially the more recent ones and those which apply to intrinsically dangerous occupations or industries, do not always impose duties which can be discharged by taking reasonably practicable measures. Rather, the duty is strict. This means that the exact wording of the demands of legislation must be complied with. Commonly used words are 'ensure', 'provide', 'make available'. Where duties, for example regarding provision of information, carrying out tests or proper health surveillance, are expressed as strict, then they *must* be complied with.

---

### EXAMPLES OF 'STRICT' DEMANDS FROM REGULATIONS

'Where it is appropriate for the protection of the health of his employees who are, or are liable to be, exposed to a substance hazardous to health, the employer *shall ensure that such employees are under suitable health surveillance.'* (COSHH Regulations Reg 11(1))

'...no means likely to ignite vapour from any highly flammable liquid *shall be present where a dangerous concentration of vapours from highly flammable liquids may reasonably be expected to be present.'* (Highly Flammable Liquids and Liquefied Petroleum Cases Regulations 1972 Reg 9 (1))

'An employer who undertakes work which may expose any of his employees to substances hazardous to health *shall provide that employee with such information*, instruction and training as is suitable and sufficient for him to know':
(i)    the risks to health created by such exposure
(ii)   the precautions which should be taken. (COSHH Regulations, Reg 12(1))

'*Effective and suitable provision shall be made to ensure* that every enclosed workplace is ventilated by a sufficient quantity of fresh or purified air.' (Workplace (Health, Safety and Welfare) Regulations 1992)

'Where a person is a display screen user, his employer *shall ensure he is provided with adequate health and safety training...*' (Health and Safety (Display Screen Equipment) Regulations 1992)

In all these situations, the employer must establish systems and follow the law precisely. The imposition of strict duties also requires that employers and others are proactive. This means that they cannot wait to see what the general or average response to an issue is; they must comply right from the outset.

---

It is therefore important that managers are well aware:

- that there are legal rules applying to specific work situations and/or activities, mainly regardless of employment sector, organisation size or work location, detailing the policy objectives and strategy of law, especially where it has European origins. UK courts and tribunals are required to reflect these objectives in their decision making. This is *not* an academic or general issue. It directly affects the way in which employers and managers are required to act;

- of the *precise* nature of the legal duties;

- of the standard of care expected, i.e. the procedures and measures which much be established and followed.

## HOW ARE SAFETY STATUTES ENFORCED?

Health and safety statutes are enforced in a number of ways. Initially, legislation concentrated on developing and enforcing law in industries and occupations of high risk, such as mines and nuclear installations. The specialised nature of this legislation meant that separate and discrete inspectorates and enforcement procedures developed.

One of the major strategies of the Health and Safety at Work Act 1974 was to provide an umbrella enforcement and policy-development organisation – the Health and Safety Executive – to ensure greater cohesion and consistency. Enforcement is undertaken by the following:

- Health and Safety Executive

- agents appointed to enforce on the HSE's behalf, e.g.:

    - Pipelines Inspectorate
    - UK Atomic Energy Authority
    - National Radiological Protection Board
    - various government departments

- local authorities

Local authorities have long had responsibility for health and safety in shops, offices, warehouses, hotels and catering premises. Following the Enforcement Authority Regulations 1989, local authorities also have responsibility for most sport, leisure and consumer activities, churches, and for health and safety aspects of the care and treatment of animals – vets, kennels etc. Environmental health officers carry out the enforcement. Workers on government-sponsored training schemes and students on work placements have their own special regulations (Health and Safety (Young Persons) Regulations 1996.

## INSPECTORS AND INSPECTIONS

Inspectors have the following powers (Section 20 HSWA):

- to enter premises at any reasonable time, or at any time of the day, if they have reason to believe a dangerous situation exists; a right to enter with a police officer if they anticipate obstruction;

- to carry out examinations, take measurements, photographs and samples;

- to arrange for the testing or dismantling of any article or substance which has caused or is likely to cause harm;

- to question relevant people;

- to inspect or take copies of books or documents which are required to be kept by law;

- to demand appropriate facilities and assistance.

The Act provides some safeguards for employers and others. An inspector must, for example, comply with a request by a person in charge of premises that he or she be present when an inspector is dismantling or testing machinery.

The inspectorates develop planned inspection programmes, targeting occupations and premises which appear to be accident prone. They react to unduly high levels of ill-health in certain occupations or organisations. This can reflect growing concerns with issues such as the so-called sick building syndrome, the impact of information technology and the influence of chemicals and gases on employee health.

Employers have to expect inspectors to be concerned with a wider range of issues than those primarily associated with machinery and substances. The number of inspections is increasing, especially of smaller organisations (those employing less than 25 people) and of public-sector employers such as universities.

## WHAT CAN INSPECTORS DO IF THERE ARE RISKS?

One of the innovations introduced by HSWA 1974 was that an effective way to bring home to employers that they needed to establish and maintain a healthy and safe workplace would be to require change, improvement in systems or, if the situation was dangerous, to shut down a workplace, part of it or a machine etc. This is clearly effective in manufacturing and service sectors where productivity and profitability are directly affected, but even in the public sector an intervention by a safety inspector can cause massive disruption and inconvenience.

### Improvement Notices
If an inspector is of the opinion that a person:

- 'is contravening one or more of the relevant statutory provisions or

- has contravened one or more of these provisions in circumstances that make it likely that the contravention will continue or be repeated'

he or she may serve an Improvement Notice (Section 21 HSWA).

There is a wide range of possible subjects for an Improvement Notice. Typical examples include upgrading safety guards, improving ventilation, lighting or the storage of equipment. In the main notices relate to equipment and buildings, but they can cover any statutory duty, for example to provide a safety policy, better safety notices or information, or a COSHH risk assessment. Inspectors can refer persons to a relevant Code of Practice but can also offer alternative ways of meeting the law's demands. Buildings which are too cold or damp could be improved by, for example, better heating, or by better ventilation and/or decoration. Today, the failure to carry out risk assessments, provide training or information is just as likely to be the subject of an Improvement Notice.

**Prohibition Notices**

This is clearly a wider and more dramatic power. A Prohibition Notice can take one of two forms – deferred and immediate prohibition.

If an inspector is of the opinion that 'any activities ... as carried on or about to be carried on... will involve risk of serious personal injury, the inspector may serve... a notice' (Section 22(2) HSWA).

A Deferred Notice will specify what must be remedied and by what time. It will 'bite', i.e. prevent an activity or use of premises if not remedied. An Immediate Notice, which can be imposed where the risk of personal injury is imminent, prevents use of equipment, the building or the whole organisation from the moment it is served.

Prohibition Notices can be served even where there is no breach of statute; risk to health or safety is the central issue. Again, although the construction industry and other areas of work prone to high accident rates figure prominently here, notices can be served to prevent work where, for example, risk assessments have not been made under COSHH Regulations or for the use of display screen equipment. Information regarding notices has to be given by inspectors to employee safety representatives.

Under the Deregulation and Contracting Out Act 1994 an imspector has to issue a 'minded to' notice before formally issuing an improvement order. This must specify what has to be done and by whom. The employer has two weeks to appeal to a panel of inspectors before formal action is taken.

## Can you appeal against statutory notices?

Persons affected can appeal to an industrial tribunal against both an Improvement and/or a Prohibition Notice. Improvement Notices are suspended during the period until the appeal is heard; Prohibition Notices continue to be operative during this period.

---

### Example – the baker's shop

Two women were employed in a small baker's shop in a town centre. The proprietor was served with an Improvement Notice to provide toilet and washing facilities at the shop for the employees. An appeal was made on the basis of the high cost and on the proximity of a particular public convenience. The industrial tribunal was also informed of the frequency over a long time span of the women's visits to the public convenience. Apparently, they made very few visits. The Improvement Notice was lifted. (unreported)

## WHAT IF YOU IGNORE THE NOTICE?

Ignoring a statutory notice is a serious matter. The person concerned can be prosecuted and fined. If there is a contravention of a Prohibition Notice, for example by continuing to use a highly dangerous substance, there is a possibility of the employer being imprisoned for up to two years (section 33(4) HSWA).

Additionally, contravention of an Improvement or Prohibition Notice can lead to the imposition by a court of a fine for each day on which the contravention continued (section 33(5) HSWA).

## PROSECUTIONS

Contravening safety legislation has always been a matter for criminal law in the UK; there are no suggestions or likelihood that it will be decriminalised. Prosecutions can be made after an inspection, accident or, as mentioned above, for non-compliance with a statutory notice. It is vital to note that, even though no one has been hurt or suffered ill health, a prosecution can be brought if there is a risk.

---

### AN EXAMPLE – LEGIONNAIRE'S DISEASE

The Science Museum in London was prosecuted due to poor maintenance standards in the heating and ventilation systems of the museum. It was successfully prosecuted under s3 HSWA even though there was no evidence that any member of the public had become ill. (*R v Board of Trustees of Science Museum*, 1994)

---

## WHAT IF SENIOR MANAGEMENT IS UNAWARE OF OR IGNORES PROBLEMS?

For a long time in UK law where an organisation (company, local authority etc.) was prosecuted for a breach of legislation, courts looked to see if the act(s) complained of were the result of a 'directing mind'. This means that prosecutions could only be successful against an organisation where senior managers were aware of or in some way caused the breach. An error or decision by a junior staff member would not make the whole organisation liable if senior managers could claim that they played no part. (The junior staff member could be personally liable, however.)

In health and safety law this approach was problematic, especially today with the emphasis of law generally on the need for effective safety management. The issue has now been considered by a law court, with an outcome which clearly establishes the ongoing and basic responsibility of senior management for health and safety.

---

### AN EXAMPLE – THE COLLAPSING STEEL PLATFORM

In July 1990, a steel platform was erected at British Steel's Sheffield plant by subcontractors. It was inadequately secured and collapsed on one of the subcontractors, killing him.

British Steel was prosecuted for a breach of s3 HSWA (failing to protect a non-employee). The company argued that it had taken 'reasonably practicable' steps in organising the work and appointing the subcontractors; it could have done no more. The argument was rejected. Health and safety law is a serious matter; it requires that all in an organisation take responsibility and there is no role for senior managers to 'opt out' and thereby protect their organisation, declared the court. To hold otherwise would encourage senior managers to turn a blind eye to issues.

Senior management, therefore, is required not only to establish procedures, here for subcontractors, but to check that the work procedures and practices they adopt are adequate and safe. (*R v British Steel*, 1995)

---

### WHEN ARE INDIVIDUAL EMPLOYEES PROSECUTED?

The simple answer is, not that often. Each year there are a number (usually around 40) of successful prosecutions against named individuals; these include company secretaries, directors and managers as well as 'ordinary' employees. Prosecutions are usually for failing to wear protective equipment, endangering others or not following safety procedures. The maximum fine per offence which can be imposed in Magistrates' Courts, or Sheriffs' Courts in Scotland, is £20,000. Where prosecutions are made before Crown Courts or equivalent, the fine is unlimited and imprisonment can be ordered in serious cases. However, multiple charges can be made and this can lead to far higher sums being imposed in aggregate.

The inspectorates are particularly severe when employees collude to break legislation, such as by removing safety guards, ignoring red/stop lights etc. The fact that this might have been done to work more quickly or meet a deadline is irrelevant. Similarly, it is irrelevant that the employee was experienced or had an excellent previous safety record.

AN EXAMPLE – THE EXPLOSION IN THE SCIENCE LABORATORY

Two students were severely injured in a laboratory at Basildon College, Essex. Their long-serving chemistry lecturer was prosecuted for breach of s7 HSWA and fined £750. The evidence was that the lecturer conducted an unauthorised experiment to make gunpowder. The components were mixed using a mortar and pestle and there was an explosion.

The incident took place at the end of the Autumn term, as a light-hearted entertainment. Nonetheless, the court considered the matter a serious breach of law. (R v Llewellyn Jones, 1993)

## WHAT OF MANSLAUGHTER?

Outside the UK it is commonplace that, if an error by, say, a coach driver, architect, ship's captain or machinist causes the death of an employee or someone else, that person is arrested and charged with manslaughter. Manslaughter is defined as causing death through gross recklessness. Breaking health and safety rules – especially being aware of major risks, such as driving with defective steering, operating a machine with no safety guard or cut-out mechanisms or providing a service for the public with no regard for safe procedures, especially emergency procedures – can amount to manslaughter.

In 1995 a landmark was reached in UK law. The manager as well as the company itself were successfully prosecuted for manslaughter as a consequence of the Lyme Bay canoeing disaster.

CASE STUDY – THE OUTDOOR PURSUITS CENTRE

In May 1993, a party of young people attended a course at the St Alban's Centre, Lyme Regis. Their week's course included canoeing. During a canoeing expedition across Lyme Bay, they got into difficulties and four young people drowned.

The evidence was that the instructors accompanying the trip were inexperienced, poorly qualified and poorly trained. The equipment was also inadequate and there was a lack of emergency equipment. All in all, there was a series of errors, poor preparation and 'cutting corners'. Furthermore, there was strong evidence that many people had warned of poor standards at the Centre and that its directors had ignored the warnings and had put economic considerations before safety. (R v Kite, 1994)

This case has been followed by several successful prosecutions for manslaughter.

Although there are potentially effective mechanisms in the Health and Safety at Work Act 1974, it must not be forgotten that, in serious situations where death or injury has occurred, organisations and/or individuals can also be charged with ordinary crimes other than manslaughter.

## ENFORCEMENT VIA CIVIL LAW

Where breach of safety law leads to death or injury to employees or to others, for example passengers or users of leisure facilities, victims can make claims for compensation in the law of negligence or for breach of statutory duty. These areas of law will be considered more fully in Chapter 5, but it remains the case that civil remedies are seen as having a major role to play in enforcing safety legislation. The adverse publicity, expense and time needed to defend claims, as well as the payment of compensation (albeit paid by insurance companies), are seen as vital sanctions.

Figure 2.1 gives a summary of enforcement mechanisms.

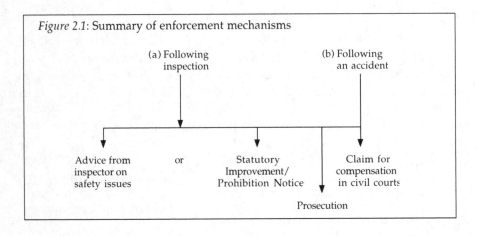

Figure 2.1: Summary of enforcement mechanisms

(a) Following inspection

(b) Following an accident

Advice from inspector on safety issues

or

Statutory Improvement/ Prohibition Notice

Claim for compensation in civil courts

Prosecution

# 3

# *Health and Safety Management and Systems*

The previous chapter considered the scope and nature of the statutory framework and its enforcement. The primary aim of that legislation is the prevention of accidents. However, analyses of the causes of accidents by the Health and Safety Executive clearly show that human error is at least a contributory factor in 90 per cent of accidents, most of which could have been prevented by effective management action.

The findings of various inquiries into recent major disasters have had considerable impact. The Fennell inquiry into the management system employed by London Underground Ltd at the time of the King's Cross disaster, the Sheen inquiry into the Zeebrugge ferry disaster, along with the Cullen inquiry into the Piper Alpha oil-rig disaster, have all emphasised the key role of safety management in accident prevention. Increasingly, the connection is being made between good management, good safety standards, good health records and good productivity, coupled with good publicity.

Therefore, there has been growing recognition in the UK that the key to good health and safety standards is good management. European legislation adopts a similar approach. Health and safety management is an important function and should have the same priority as product development, business policy, financial planning etc. Ideally, it should be located within the human resources management function, although many organisations either develop a specialist health and safety function or combine it with management of plant and equipment. There is no single right answer.

However, law requires the following of all employing organisations:

- evidence that health and safety is taken seriously, especially at the most senior level;

- adequate and appropriate resources, skills and experience devoted to health and safety;

- clear lines of managerial responsibility and accountability;

- that all employees and, if appropriate, non-employees, such as contractors, self-employed persons and staff supplied by employment agencies, should be aware of health and safety responsibilities.

## WHAT IS INCLUDED IN HEALTH AND SAFETY MANAGEMENT?

At least the following:

- a clear, robust health and safety policy and ensuring it is adequately resourced;

- arrangements for the purchase, modification and maintenance of premises;

- arrangements for the purchase, testing, monitoring, maintenance and repair of equipment;

- management of hazardous substances, to include their transportation and storage;

- use of information systems, instruction and supervision of employees; safety training;

- effective safety monitoring and review;

- mechanisms for liaison, information, consultation and protection of all employees, especially new employees and those employed by subcontractors, agency temps etc., as well as visitors to premises and members of the public;

- health surveillance and welfare systems.

## WHAT ARE THE NEW MANAGEMENT TOPICS?

Two particular issues stand out which both require new and appropriate management strategies. The first is recent change in the nature of many employing organisations, especially regarding moves towards decentralisation and therefore increasing autonomy for smaller work units. Even more important has been the fragmentation of the workforce through the increased reliance on temporary, casual, self-employed and agency staff and the flexible workforce more generally. Particularly significant has been the escalation in the use of subcontractors, especially in the public sector. The growing complexity of the workforce may increase difficulties in maintaining efficient communications systems; and supervision in these new circumstances is an area to which considerable attention must be given. Law is emphasising it; so must management systems.

The second issue of growing importance is that of occupational health, especially for the more vulnerable sections of the workforce, and, indeed, the health of the wider community. Increasing attention is being paid to the impact of industrial and other activities on people in neighbouring areas, customers and, for example, members of the travelling public. The Health and Safety Executive has itself drawn attention to all these issues and the law courts have entertained a widening range of legal actions, including cases on passive smoking and stress.

## WHAT DO THE MANAGEMENT OF HEALTH AND SAFETY AT WORK REGULATIONS 1992 REQUIRE?

The key tasks are as follows.

**To establish procedures for the effective 'planning, organisation, control, monitoring and review of health and safety'** (Reg 4)

Advice on this from the HSE is encapsulated in Figure 3.1: management tasks start from the bottom and work upwards. All these stages require careful preparation and, most importantly, effective and constant delivery.

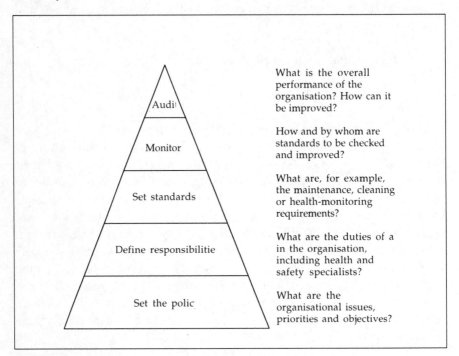

These tasks have relevance to all aspects of the organisation's work. The law requires that individual areas of the workplace, such as safety of stairs, lifts, walkways, car parks etc., should have the triangle of procedures applied to them, as well as the organisation itself in delivering in its legal duties as a whole.

### EXAMPLE – A PUBLIC LIBRARY

For example, taking the key tasks in order, a public library would need to demonstrate at least the following;

**Setting a policy** might involve not only establishing a framework for employees, but also ensuring that there are adequate protection, facilities and information for members of the public and visitors from outside the library.

**Defining the responsibilities for health and safety** would involve setting up a management structure, identifying and meeting the need for specialist advice/support, ensuring that all staff are aware of their own duties, backed up, as appropriate, by disciplinary rules, appraisal and pay systems. For example, what should be the role of the chief librarian? The role of occupational health specialists and the human resources/personnel function would need to be clarified, as would, for example, responsibilities for fires/emergencies. Job descriptions might need to be amended.

**Setting standards** might involve attention to performance management/disciplinary rules for individuals, but also clear rules for maintenance, surveillance, inspections etc. Library equipment purchased needs to meet quality standards. Health targets should be set and absence/illness rates reduced, along with accident/incident rates.

**Monitoring standards** is likely to involve the library setting up or reconsidering a safety committee. But what should be its terms of reference, membership and administration? What else would need to be done? Could readers' surveys include health and safety questions? Who should be inspecting premises? What are the arrangements for reporting faults?

An **audit** might involve bringing in a specialist auditor to check that the system as a whole is efficient and to suggest improvements.

*It should be noted that using specialists/consultants on behalf of the organisation does not absolve the employer from legal responsibility or delegate that responsibility. You are only as good as your consultant: the law sees the employer, not the consultant, as liable if anything goes wrong.*

**To 'make a suitable and sufficient assessment of risks to the health and safety of employees' and to 'persons not in his employment' (Reg 3)**
The task at the heart of all modern health and safety legislation is that of assessing all potential workplace risks. The assessment has to be done in a formal way and the outcome has to be 'in writing' and to record any group of employees 'especially at risk' where more than five are employed.

Any existing risk assessment also has to be reviewed if 'there is reason to suspect it is no longer valid' or 'there has been a significant change in the matters to which it relates' (Reg 3(3)). This clearly applies to situations which involve new machinery, refurbished premises or new work processes. It should also apply where staff numbers are reduced or increased in the same work area, a building previously occupied alone is now shared, a night shift is introduced or working hours changed significantly. All organisational and workforce changes will almost invariably have a knock-on effect on risk assessments. A new risk assessment should therefore automatically accompany the change.

The law's strategy is to put employing organisations on alert. They should find out what the risks are to which their workforce and others are exposed. They must not wait until an accident occurs before recognising that they have a problem to deal with. In the past, if one or two people fell down some stairs because of a loose carpet, poor lighting, lack of a handrail etc., it was clear that the stairs were unsafe. However, law now requires an assessment of the risk of slipping or falling even before anyone is injured.

Law also implies that risk assessments should be done with an open mind. For example, an organisation in financial services might assume that the major workplace risks for its staff are from use of display screen equipment (RSI, eye strain etc.). However, in reality, far more important might be risks from passive smoking, fatigue or stress. The last might be a risk because the management policy has been to reduce staff numbers, increase both workload and working hours, and generally develop an aggressive and unsupportive culture.

Each recent piece of health and safety legislation, to a greater or lesser extent, has required risk assessment. This may be in connection with lifting loads, using machinery, using chemical or other substances, working in a noisy environment, or because a woman is pregnant and may now be vulnerable to other risks such as from lifting, excess heat or cold or overcrowding.

The law calls for 'adequate' risk assessments. But how do managers know when an assessment is 'adequate'? Doubts may arise as to its scope (might some risks have been left out?) or its thoroughness (have all risks been assessed properly, i.e. how risky does something have to be before it is recorded?). At the time of writing these questions remain problematic because case law has not yet evolved to provide clear pointers.

However, virtually all sets of UK regulations contain either an Advisory Code of Practice (ACOP) or Guidance Notes which provide useful information as to how the task should be done. In addition, many health and safety consultancies offer advice or will carry out the assessments, although in the main risk assessments are better done by in-house staff.

General advice suggests that employers should, first, identify that there is a risk of some level in the workplace, e.g. from fire, violent attacks by the public, falling down a lift shaft, inhalation of dust etc. Then two further questions arise. First, how frequently does the risk arise – hourly, monthly, yearly? Secondly, if an incident/accident/illness were to occur, how likely is it that it would be serious? Is the danger of death or major injury, or of a cut, bruise etc.? Figure 3.2 sets out a simple methodology for the task.

Numbers 1–4 provide a gradation. For example, 4 on the vertical axis might be 'death' and 4 on the horizontal axis 'continuous'; 1 on the ver-

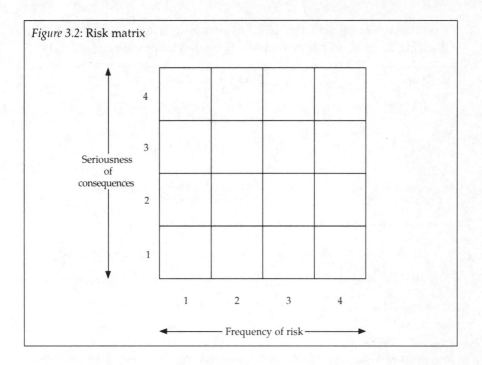

*Figure 3.2*: Risk matrix

tical axis might be 'alarm/concern', 1 on the horizontal axis 'annually or extremely rarely'.

Someone working with explosives might well have a score of 16, multiplying the two axis scores, because the risk of an explosion is both constant and life threatening. The measures which the employer needs to take to protect the employee should be consistent with that score; i.e. they should be significant.

The matrix is not helpful in all cases, for example it would not be applicable where you have a major risk, say of falling from a height. However, because few people work on roofs or at that height, the chances of a fall happening remain slight. It is difficult to judge, in these circumstances, whether all the possible protective measures (scaffolding, hoists, safety harnesses etc.) should be taken. The law's view would probably be that employers should have carried out a proper assessment, put it in the context of past experience and adopted a procedure which minimised the risk. Employing a subcontractor to do the work does not absolve the employer of responsibility.

The process of risk assessment clearly requires access to and use of organisational data. This data needs to cover what risks there are or might be and to identify who is at risk. Is it only employees? Members of the public, patients, school pupils etc.?

Risk assessment will probably require examination of, at least, the following in order to get a complete overview of organisational risks:

| Topic | Examples of questions to apply |
| --- | --- |
| Use of premises | Who uses them and for what purpose? How frequently? |
| Equipment purchasing procedures | What purchased and by whom? |
| Equipment use | Who uses it? Are they experienced, trained, supervised? |
| Use of subcontractors | What is done, by whom, when? |
| Working practices/times | Where are people working; for how long? |
| Labour-use strategies | Are part-timers or agency staff used? |
| Staff health | When checked, with what results? |

**Respond to risk assessments by ensuring appropriate 'protective and preventive measures'** (Reg 4)

This is also referred to as risk management, although, as has been considered previously, the law's current view is that the employer's aim should be to eliminate risk and only take certain protective measures as a last resort, such as providing goggles, masks, or even training in, say, how to lift loads. Other avenues should first have been explored, such as how to avoid individuals lifting loads at all by substituting lifting machinery or changing workshop design.

It is suggested that an appropriate response to any given risk assessment, e.g. one which has identified the risk from lifting of back injury or other musculo-skeletal problem, would be the following. Responses should be considered in this order; the next step should only be considered if the previous one is impossible or impracticable.

**Step 1** *Eliminate* the risk, e.g. introduce hoists or belts and the like so no manual handling is required.

**Step 2** *Substitute* the risk, e.g. replace a trolley with a moving belt.

**Step 3** *Contain* the risk, e.g. ensure that only loads of a certain weight are manually lifted or only by two people.

**Step 4** *Protect*, e.g. provide proper training, supervision and support.

In any given situation the essence of the law's demands is that all options should be explored and considered **'with transparency'**. This European concept implies that employers should not only undertake these various tasks associated with risk management, but should be able to demonstrate that they did so and defend their strategy, if necessary, to a safety inspector.

It is important to note that Regulation 3 also requires 'every self-employed person' to make a risk assessment of their own risks at work and to others. It is therefore legitimate to ask, say, freelance staff, contractors and even 'casuals' to assess their own risks. If they cannot, that might well indicate that they should not be used by the employing organisation. It should also be noted that, even though a self-employed person assesses the risks to themselves, that does not absolve the employing organisation from its own duties regarding health and safety.

---

RESPONDING TO RISK ASSESSMENTS: A SECONDARY SCHOOL

Blackstone School had undertaken a risk assessment on its premises. This indicated that poorly lit and narrow staircases created a significant risk of trips and falls, especially at lesson changeover times. One of the steps was badly worn; a piece of concrete became detached, leaving the step dangerous. The safety manager decided that there was a significant risk of injury, but was faced with a dilemma. Should he close off the staircase? Should he put up a warning sign? Should staff members closely supervise pupils? How should he respond? Each option was explored in turn. Closing the staircase would put excess pressure on the other usable staircase at the other end of the corridor. It was explored whether changeovers could be staggered, but this was impossible. Warning signs were considered, but were likely to be ignored. In the end it was thought that the best option would be to keep the staircase open and erect signs, but to use two members of staff – one at the top, one at the foot of the stairs – to warn pupils verbally of the danger and generally discipline the movement of pupils. **There were no accidents.**

---

**To ensure that employees are 'provided with such health surveillance as is appropriate'** (Reg 5)

This management task will be considered more fully in Chapter 6. Effective in-house or outsourced medical and counselling procedures need to be present. The Management Regulations reinforce other legislation, for example relating to noise, hazardous substances, biological agents (bacteria, viruses etc.) use of display screens (eyesight tests etc.), which requires specific tests and procedures to be followed.

Occupational health is of growing and considerable importance – not least because of cost implications (see Chapter 1).

Law does not require all organisations to employ full-time occupational health practitioners or that the people they use hold professional qualifications, e.g. as an optician, physiotherapist or psychologist. However, they do have to be 'competent', as judged by training, experience and abilities. Contracting out for such skills is obviously acceptable, especially for smaller organisations or those with a generally low level of work risks, but the choice of contractor and the nature and quality of service they provide still has to be 'appropriate'. Once again, it will be the employer in court if anything goes wrong.

## WHO PROVIDES THE SPECIALIST ADVICE?

Regulation 6 requires every employer to 'appoint one or more competent persons to assist him in undertaking the measures he needs... To comply with legislation, such persons must have time available for them to fulfil their functions and the means at their disposal [should be] adequate.' Such a person must also be provided with adequate information, in particular about people on fixed-term contracts and supplied by employment businesses (agencies) (Reg 6(4)(b)).

The 'competent persons' need not have any prescribed qualification but they must have 'sufficient training and experience or knowledge and other qualities' for health and safety demands.

So employers must use safety specialists, but these can be employees or consultants. Much will depend on the size and nature of the organisation. There must, however, be a named individual with appropriate skills to 'assist'. It is extremely important to note that the individual is there to support the organisation, not to be a substitute for managerial efficiency in the organisation itself. It is clearly helpful if the named individual holds a qualification accredited by the National Council for Vocational Qualifications or equivalent.

It is essential that the person(s) appointed should have sufficient information, resources and access to decision makers. Duties under the legislation are not discharged by appointing, say, a safety manager and marginalising them in the organisation. They must have clout!

## OTHER KEY MANAGEMENT TASKS

### HEALTH AND SAFETY INFORMATION

Many research studies have highlighted ignorance and apathy as major causal factors in the continuing high level of accidents. Many accidents are caused primarily or solely by employees through carelessness or occasionally deliberate acts. Information is vital not only in highlighting or reinforcing safety issues but also in changing the 'climate' of an organisation. A visit to premises with yellowing or defaced safety instructions will give a clear impression of that organisation's safety attitudes and of management laxity.

The Management Regulations (MHSWR) 1992, Regs 8 and 9, reinforcing earlier UK legislation, make specific reference to the provision of information in two situations:

- For employees, on their risks to health and safety (arising from risk assessments), the nature of preventive and protective measures, evacuation/emergency procedures, safety specialists in the organisation and the nature of any special risks.

- For non-employees, regarding special risks.

This is an important aspect of law, as it is one which reflects the 'new' health and safety law's response that the greater the risk(s), the greater the attention must be given. Non-employees (third-party workers), such as the self-employed, visitors and workers employed by subcontractors, are likely to be less familiar with the workplace and its procedures, and thus even more in need of clear and helpful information.

MHSWR require the 'exchange' as well as provision of health and safety information where workplaces are shared (e.g. a multi-occupancy office block or construction site with several employers working on it) or non-employees are using it. In particular, such third-party workers need adequate information on risks. The duty applies to agency, freelance and subcontracted staff, for example (Regs 9 and 10).

Under the Health and Safety Information for Employees Regulations 1989, there are other specific requirements for information regarding health and safety. It has to be provided by means of posters or leaflets in a form prescribed by the Health and Safety Executive, copies of which are available from HMSO. The Regulations require the name of the enforcing authority and the address of the employment medical advisory service to be written in the appropriate space on the poster.

These Regulations provide for the minimum amount of information employers should provide; often more could be included regarding specific hazards or rules.

## WRITTEN SAFETY POLICIES

Section 2(3) of MHSWR imposes a duty on employers of five or more persons to prepare and distribute a written statement of safety policy. Information can be obtained from Leaflet HSC6 *Guidance Notes on Employers' Policy Statements for Health and Safety at Work* and *Writing Your Health and Safety Policy Statement*.

A policy should cover at least the three following areas:

* A general statement of the organisation's overall attitude to safety. This should identify priorities and aspects of special concern. It should avoid blandness and provide examples of special concerns, as well as precise reasons for safety and health being important to the organisation, e.g. links with productivity, effective recruitment and employee well-being.

* Clarification of safety management structures in the organisation, to include senior management responsible by name, role of safety representatives and safety committees, safety specialists, occupational health practitioners etc. This can be done diagrammatically.

* Practical arrangements for health and safety, such as information regarding emergencies, accident reporting, health surveillance and fire procedures.

The document must be regularly, probably annually, revised and reissued. It will need to reflect recent and emerging legal and practical issues and be applicable to a wide range of people. Long-standing employees will often have information which is out of date and the organisation will need to keep them in mind to avoid complacency.

The document can be usefully tested out on someone unfamiliar with the organisation to see if it is clear and helpful. If so, it can be confidently issued to non-employees such as agency temps.

The policy can have added to it other workplace policies, for example on sexual harassment, smoking and AIDS. Colour coding and loose binding can help to make the total 'package' attractive, readab.. anu capable of selective distribution to third parties such as subcontractors.

## SAFETY CONSULTATION

A matter which is of growing importance in a European context is consultation with employees (not just their union representatives) on both planned changes and ongoing issues. Consultation should take place *before* a change or development and should be a true dialogue. These ideas carry over into health and safety.

A particular issue in the UK had been that the Safety Representatives and Safety Committees Regulations 1977 limited the obligation to consult and set up a committee to employers who formally recognise unions for these purposes. Only an estimated 10 per cent of employers have committees and, due to the decline in trade union membership and collective agreements, the numbers formally consulting over health and safety have similarly reduced.

It is clear that this legislation was inadequate in European legal terms. The Health and Safety (Consultation with Employees) Regulations 1996 require effective procedures for consultation, even where there are no trade unions. Employers can choose whether to continue to recognise a union(s) or seek elected representatives.

Prudent employers will ensure that they do have adequate health and safety consideration procedures (departmental meetings, consultative committees, staff associations), even beyond the strict statutory requirements.

## SAFETY REPRESENTATIVES

Safety representatives are employees familiar with the workplace who may be appointed by a recognised trade union(s) or elected by employees generally. They have powers to:

- investigate hazards and accidents;
- investigate complaints;
- investigate reportable accidents, the workplace and safety documents;
- represent groups of employees to the employer;
- attend meetings of the safety committee, or similar.

Ideally, as indicated above, information and consultation should be undertaken by the employer as a matter of course and should precede the introduction of new work machinery or processes. Meetings and discussions, for example between safety managers and safety representatives, should avoid over-formality, and a system should be established which is responsive to complaints and problems.

## Safety Committees

Where requested by at least two safety representatives, the employer must establish a committee after consultation and within three months of the request. The employer can determine the committee's composition, frequency of meetings, agendas and chairing of meetings. Given that it is largely a matter of discretion how the employer fulfils the statutory duty, it may be useful to pose the following questions:

- What is the precise role of the committee – is it to discuss, to inform, or does it have executive powers?

- What is the relationship between the committee and the safety manager and/or safety officer?

- How is membership of the committee decided? Is it a cross-section of the workforce, or an expert group? What role do individuals play on the committee? Does the membership reflect all relevant interests, for example health and welfare interests?

- How are decisions made as to the chairing of the committee and items for the agenda? Is it primarily a 'talking shop' with items routinely put on the agenda, or is it there to deal with emergency and emerging issues? Can it actually develop policy?

- How does one assess whether the committee is effective? How are proposals for changes in role and/or composition arrived at?

- Does the committee initiate safety exercises such as questionnaires, or evaluate accident records? If not, why not?

- How does it fit within the management structure and management information systems more generally?

Important also is the question of whether the committee's remit and composition effectively represent the wider workforce. Is it possible, for example, to encourage participation by part-timers and fixed-term employees whose perceptions and concerns might be different from the permanent full-timer? What of external employees such as employees of a subcontractor on a long contract for services?

## SAFETY MONITORING

As considered earlier, employers are required to identify 'danger' and assess the 'risk' which danger creates. An unfenced floor opening or a badly worn stair will constitute a danger; effective responses to that danger will relate to the number, type and frequency of people exposed to the danger. At the same time there is a need to alert and educate employees as to the nature and scale of risks and to encourage an appropriate response. How can organisations ensure that they have identified and responded to dangers? They might:

- Note carefully the outcome of the meetings of the health and safety committee and wider consultation.

- Undertake safety surveys and tours which might provide detailed information, as well as using unscheduled visits or examinations.

- Employ safety audits. These can vary from organisation to organisation and can be developed on an organisation-specific basis or can use a proprietary scheme. The British Safety Council and the Royal Society for the Prevention of Accidents (RoSPA) market widely applicable schemes. Audits have two purposes:

  - to assess whether behaviour at the workplace conforms to legal and organisational rules;
  - to assess the adequacy of organisational rules and procedures. It is crucial that audits cover not only the 'hardware' in terms of plant and machinery but also address matters of training, management, supervision and consultation.

Although audits differ in terms of reporting systems, the important issue for law is that there is an effective response to an audit, especially where it has identified problems. The audit may have alerted organisations to specific issues. If this is the case the law will now require management to react; turning a blind eye is always frowned on. Organisations should:

- use safety inspections by appropriately qualified professionals, especially where there are particular issues, e.g. over display screen equipment;

- incorporate safety issues in staff management and appraisal systems;

- systematically evaluate the safety record of subcontractors and other non-employee groups. This requires a clear view of safety standards prior to the contract being undertaken, responses to incidents and dangers, and incorporation of safety terms in the contract which spell out the consequences of safety breaches. These might include:
  - the right to terminate the contract;
  - the right to demand the recall to the subcontractor of 'dangerous staff' who create risks or hazards;
  - financial compensation.

Evaluation of subcontractors is vital in the light of the emphasis given to it by MHSWR. Information and communication systems enable performance and the contract itself to be kept under review.

---

### EXAMPLE – AN ACCIDENT CAUSED BY VOMIT

A south London hospital had recently employed contract cleaners. There was a build-up of resentment between nursing and cleaning staff and a number of small accidents and incidents over allegedly poor cleaning standards. One day there was a serious accident when a patient slipped on vomit on a ward floor which had not been cleaned up. Investigations revealed that, although the hospital manager was aware of difficulties with the cleaning contract, there was no systematic monitoring of contract performance and no clear procedure for responding to diffculties. (Leighton, P, *Sub-contracting for services*, Report to ILO, 1985)

---

### DEALING WITH IRREGULAR OR INFREQUENT PROBLEMS

Hazards or dangers which are less regular must also be planned for, monitored and managed effectively. Clearly, this applies to first aid, fire and other emergency procedures so that all personnel are aware of how to enlist help and avoid additional risks. Safety systems must also anticipate the presence of people less familiar with the workplace or, indeed, members of the public. However, problems or difficulties can crop up which place employees in a dilemma. A vehicle may become dangerous,

---

### EXAMPLE – THE REVERSING LORRY

It is generally recognised that reversing a vehicle, especially a large one, is a difficult manoeuvre. It is advisable that, in addition to reversing lights, bleepers and adequate mirrors, a banksman (lookout) should be used. In this case a lorry driver, without an assistant, reversed his lorry in torrential rain, where visibility was very poor. He crushed to death a female employee of the company to which he was delivering goods; the delivery company and the company where the incident occurred were both successfully prosecuted.

The delivery company should have provided a banksman but, failing that, should have given clear guidance to drivers as to what they should do in very adverse weather conditions. Summon help? Deliver the goods in a different way? What the driver should not have done was take a chance. The woman's employer should have ensured that premises were safe and that there was no 'mingling' of vehicles and pedestrians. (*R v*

---

the weather deteriorate severely, a gas leak cause a building to become hazardous or a fellow employee may become unable to work. It is essential that employees are clear how to respond and whom to contact. They must not take risks or add to existing risks. Managers also need to know how effective their systems are.

## SAFETY TRAINING AND SUPERVISION

Attention to training and supervision in safety management has grown in recent years; it will need to develop further, not least because of the high priority given to these areas by European law. Training has to be provided for those whose work has obvious risks, those who work with dangerous equipment or those who require instructions for new machinery. Training and instruction have to be provided so as to ensure the health and safety at work of employees (section 2(2)(c) HSWA). Regulation 11 of MHSWR emphasises this duty.

Regulation 11 specifies training in the following situations:

- for new recruits;

- when employees are exposed to new risks because they have changed their job/role;

- when new equipment, new technology or a new work system is introduced.

In addition, training has to be repeated 'periodically' and be 'adapted' to take into account new circumstances. It must take place in working hours – including for part-time, home-based or temporary staff.

It is important to note that, when tasks are being allocated to employees, their 'capabilities as regards health and safety' should be taken into account. If they have a physical or psychological difficulty the employer must recognise this. This measure is reinforced by the Disability Discrimination Act 1995. It means, in effect, that work must be fitted to the worker, not vice versa!

There is also a need for safety and health awareness training if the intentions of legislation are to be realised. Training in recognising and reporting dangers (a specific duty on employees from MHSWR Reg 12(2)), in how to respond to emergencies and to encourage individual responsibility more generally, is not very common but is equally vital to comply fully with the law. In addition, instruction and training must be provided for non-employees such as agency temps and should be part of their induction package. Contracts with subcontractors must also require that their employees are properly trained and are familiar with the layout and facilities of the host workplace. Attention must be paid to flexible and accessible forms of training. Self-learning packages, videos etc. are available or can be devised.

Safety supervision is also vital, not only to monitor safety in a broader sense, but to ensure high standards and to make the connection more generally between disciplinary procedures and safety. Breaches of safety rules must not be seen as 'lesser offences' than, for example, dishonesty or absenteeism. The Employment Rights Act 1996 does not require communication of safety disciplinary rules in writing. However, there is nothing to prevent their inclusion in employment contracts.

Safety supervision is clearly more complex yet equally important where there are non-employees and members of the public on the premises. Contracts with agencies, labour-only subcontractors or contractors and consultants should allow the host employer to have a key role in the supervision of non-employees.

---

### EXAMPLE FROM CASE LAW

A worker, a self-employed subcontractor in the timber industry, was concerned about the odours from glues he was required to use. He complained. Nothing was done. When he complained again his contract was terminated. He claimed under TURER 1993 and won. It was not relevant that he was apparently self-employed. (*Harris v Southern Timber*, 1994)

It may be useful to pose the following questions:

- Are safety issues an integral part of managerial and supervisory appraisal systems?

- Are the managers responsible for devising contracts with agencies, contractors etc. fully aware of the safety issues and able to integrate them in the contracts?

- Are all new employees and non-employees aware of safety issues, properly trained and subject to appropriate safety supervision?

- Do disciplinary procedures respond appropriately to breaches of safety rules and poor practices?

- Is there a tightening up of disciplinary and supervisory procedures following an accident or incident? Is the situation reviewed, for example one year on?

## VICTIMISATION: THE NEW HEALTH AND SAFETY RIGHT

As noted above, under MHSWR Reg 12 employees have a specific legal duty to report health and safety shortfalls at their employing organisation. If they do complain, what happens if they are dismissed or are otherwise treated badly by management?

The European Framework Directive on Health and Safety in 1989 recognised that, if health and safety is to be taken seriously, there has to be protection for 'whistle-blowers'. The UK was required to ensure adequate protection for those with health and safety concerns. Section 100 of the Employment Rights Act 1996 covers this now (it was previously dealt with under the Trade Union Reform and Employment Rights Act 1993 (TURER). If an employee, regardless of length of service, is dismissed in connection with health and safety matters, e.g. refusing to work on a dangerous machine or to drive a vehicle with defective brakes, the dismissal is automatically unfair. The employer's only 'defence' is that the decision to refuse to work was 'unreasonable in the circumstances', i.e. the employee should have followed recommended procedures and, had this been done, he or she would not have been faced with this dilemma.

Alternatively, if the employer's response is to cause the employee in question to suffer a 'detriment' (no promotion, no bonus), compensation can be claimed from an industrial tribunal.

## ACCIDENT, DISEASE AND OCCURRENCE REPORTING

There is a front-line legal duty to report specified incidents, but beyond that good safety management should develop not only effective reporting procedures but adequate responses. The Reporting of Injuries, Diseases and Dangerous Occurrences Regulations (RIDDOR) 1985 (as amended 1995) set out the circumstances where reporting must take place, including the question of who was injured, e.g. employee, self-employed. Figure 3.3 details the basic requirements for reporting injuries at work. It is important to note that injuries caused through violence must now be reported if they lead to over three days' absence.

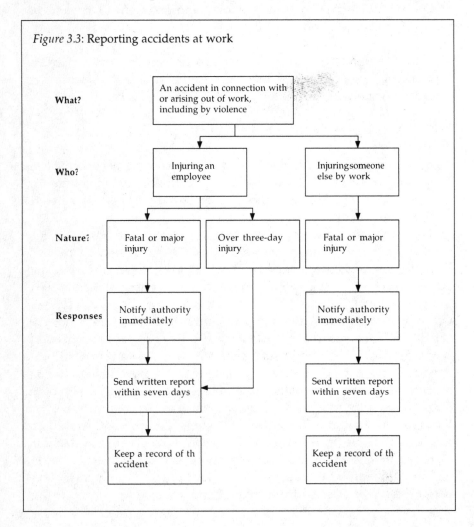

*Figure 3.3*: Reporting accidents at work

The responsibility for reporting requires users of contractors or self-employed people to report some incidents.

The main changes introduced by RIDDOR 1995 include:

- the obligation to report the death of any person as a result of a work accident, whether or not they are at work when they die;

- 'accidents' now include acts of violence;

- reportable 'major injuries' are refined and updated (Schedule 1);

- reportable 'dangerous occurrences' are refined and updated (Schedule 2) – included are transport accidents, explosions and gas leaks;

- reportable 'diseases' are refined and updated (Schedule 3) – they include illnesses caused by biological agents such as rabies, hepatitis, brucellosis.

## CASE STUDY: DEVELOPING EFFECTIVE SAFETY MANAGEMENT

This case study describes how one major UK employer responded to legal demands for effective health and safety management. The account is drawn from the organisation's documentation, interviews with key managers and knowledge of training initiatives and programmes.

BACS Limited (formerly known as Bankers Automated Clearing Service) employs approximately 500 employees of whom around 19 per cent are female. Its headquarters are in north-west London, with two other premises. The nature of its business requires the organisation to be highly efficient and responsive and to use information technology effectively. It is a fast-moving business in a competitive market. It also has a need for high security levels.

In 1993, when a new chief executive, Mr Younger, joined the organisation, BACS had a number of committees which defined policy priorities and which also developed the policies themselves. Health and safety was one such committee, along with quality, security, engineering and projects.

Health and safety had been identified as a priority area in 1993 for several compelling reasons. First, there was awareness of the new 'Six Pack' of regulations, implemented on 1 January 1993. Second, the banking industry has a strong tradition of compliance with law. Third, the organisation was well aware of the possibility of legal claims from employees which might be suffering from RSI and the likely attendant adverse publicity.

Given the organisation's strong commitment to professionalism in management, BACS embarked on a strategy to put in place effective health and safety management.

### The challenges

Bringing health and safety issues to centre stage required a review of current organisational structures, including the committee structure. There was recognition that there had to be rapid change. Although there was corporate recognition that health and safety management and standards had to improve, current management and policy-development structures did not appear to deliver the necessary changes. The health and safety committee was relatively low key and largely dealt with complaints and short-term problems. The health and safety culture had to change so that all individuals felt they had a part to play in generating and implementing health and safety progress. This was carried out by the creation of a specialist safety post and extensive training of staff in their general health and safety responsibility and also in their particular specialist roles; for example risk assessment, evacuation warden duty etc. The support of top management was widely accepted to be key to success.

### Change in mission statement

Consistent with the strategy of putting health and safety centre stage, it was recognised that the existing mission statement required review. BACS' mission was to be a 'secure, reliable, cost effective national electronic fund company'. Security was given prominence. In 1993, a commitment to health and safety was added to the mission – indeed, it was to be the subject of annual reports to BACS' board.

These developments helped put health and safety at the heart of BACS' core activities, backed up by constant input of legal demands. This, importantly, was balanced by awareness-raising initiatives for the staff generally, including a brief input on its importance immediately prior to staff presentations.

Important also at this stage was the commitment of human resources specialists. This served to emphasise the 'people' as opposed to 'property' aspects of health and safety.

Good health and safety management by individual managers was rewarded. At the same time, managers assumed accountability for health and safety standards in their areas.

### What were the priority topics?

Within two years the emphasis had switched from health and safety implementation by a few to implementation by the many. Risk assessments were carried out by trained employee assessors of display screen work and manual handling. It quickly became apparent that health problems were significant, with several musculo-skeletal problems and some stress-related illnesses. The risks to health had also been assessed and this was a more complex and difficult process. Indeed, one manager commented that these health and safety changes acted 'for the first time as a change agent for the culture of the organisation itself' – they were a catalyst. They challenged traditional work practices and even the organisational culture, which was one of long hours, commitment and reluctance to see the downside of pressure.

### What procedures and initiatives were put in place?

The management of health and safety was seen as a matter to which all employees had to contribute. It was not to be left to the specialists or the HRM function. Policy statements, booklets and publicity material were developed, along with an in-house health and safety newsletter, backed up by a safety audit and an extensive training programme of all supervisory and managerial staff.

The focus of the training has been not so much on the technical aspects of health and safety or indeed on the legal rules, but on requiring managers to take ownership of faults and problems. Training also highlighted the fact that risk assessments were just one staging post; that key to effective management are constant vigilance, awareness of communication systems and the integration of health, safety and welfare issues in all decision making.

**The costs and the benefits**
Throughout this process BACS has had a commitment to careful costing of the new health and safety systems and their management. This is reckoned to be 0.25 per cent of running costs per annum or, in 1994, £70,000 per annum inclusive of internal and external costs. This is seen as an investment.

What have been the measurable benefits? They have included lower building cleaning costs and improved staff relations.

**Other outcomes**
Knowledge and awareness of health and safety issues have grown and established a foundation from which other initiatives have developed, for example to control excess noise, deal with the safe circulation of traffic on the premises and to improve personal health, increase staff empowerment and use innovative methods in training.

# 4

# *Safety Legislation – Specific Duties*

Chapter 3 considered legal duties in relation to safety management. This chapter deals with the 'nuts and bolts' of safety legislation, including duties in relation to premises, equipment, materials etc., but also for some work activities such as handling heavy loads, use of display screen equipment and using contractors, especially for construction and maintenance work.

The reason these activities have specific duties attached to them is because research indicates that they are major causes of accidents and ill-health. Back injuries, musculo-skeletal problems (including repetitive strain injury – RSI) eye strain and stress disorders are widespread across Europe and cause major losses of productivity as well as injury and illness.

The law, taken from European directives, broadly adopts the strategies set out in Chapter 3, i.e. risk assessment and risk minimisation through preventive measures such as training, maintenance, supervision and improved equipment, monitoring and review.

## SAFE PREMISES AND STRUCTURES

The rules applicable to safe premises are obtained from a variety of sources, including:

- Health and Safety at Work Act 1974 section 2(2)(d)
  'So far as is reasonable as regards any place of work under the employer's control, the maintenance of it in a condition that is safe and without risks to health and the provision and maintenance of access and egress from it that are safe and without risks to health.'

- The Factories Act 1961 and the Offices, Shops and Railway Premises Act 1963
  These statutes provide detail on specific issues for the majority of workplaces.

- Industry- or occupation-specific regulations
  These set down particular occupations, for example, the Construction (Working Places) Regulations 1966.

- Occupiers' liability legislation
  This establishes general standards and provides compensation for injury due to the state of premises.

- Workplace Health, Safety and Welfare Regulations 1992
  This covers safety standards at any workplace, including circumstances where the employee works at home if the employer has 'control', for example by prescribing the content and layout of a home workstation. It covers lifts, car parks, sports and eating facilities, as well as the quality of working areas. It was implemented following a European directive on workplace standards.

### MAJOR DUTIES REGARDING WORKPLACES

The Workplace Health, Safety and Welfare Regulations 1992, along with their Approved Code of Practice, apply to virtually all places where people work in the UK, including public transport. The regulations do cover hotels and nursing homes but exclude ships, construction sites and outdoor agriculture, which are the subject of specialist regulations. There are references to s2 of the Health and Safety at Work Act 1974 but these regulations are more explicit and detailed.

The regulations are very 'person specific', i.e. their main objective is to ensure that people using workplaces are safe and healthy and that they receive adequate welfare provision.

The regulations affect the design, cleanliness and appropriateness of the building for work. The standard applied is generally one of strict liability, i.e. the employer must comply with the demands of law – 'reasonable' compliance is not adequate.

The key topics covered by the Workplace Regulations are as follows.

### Room dimensions and space

'Every room where persons work shall have sufficient floor area, height and unoccupied space for purposes of health, safety and welfare.' (Reg 10)

The essence here is that people should have adequate space to work and to move around. Each person should have at least 11 cubic metres in which to work. This is an absolute minimum and where offices are high, or there are many cupboards, bookshelves etc., more space will be required.

### Workstations and seating

Regulation 11 requires that:

'Every work station shall be so arranged that it is suitable both for any person at work in the workplace who is likely to work at that work station and for any work the undertaking of which is likely to be done there.'

The essence of this provision is that workstations and the workplace generally have to be designed for individual employees, including those with disabilities. Seats and footrests have to be provided (Reg 11(3)(4)) and adapted to the individual. The law recognises here that poorly designed workplaces which ignore good ergonomics can lead to problems, especially where work is repetitive and where display screen equipment is used.

### Floors, traffic routes and their organisation

One of the most common causes of accidents is poorly designed floor space and/or poor procedures for traffic management. People crushed on staircases, struck by cars and delivery vehicles or faced with poorly designed or maintained stairs, corridors, passages etc. are major contributors to accident statistics. The law accepts that slips, trips and falls are the major risks and that the failure to separate out vehicular from pedestrian traffic is especially hazardous. Regulation 12 states:

'(1)   Every floor in every workplace and the surface of every traffic route in a workplace shall be of a construction such that the floor or surface of the traffic route is suitable for the purpose for which it is used.'

The regulations then deal with specific requirements for obstruction-free passages and areas and a design which aids movement, such as the provision of handrails, suitable gradients, adequate drainage and the need to ensure that surfaces are slip resistant.

A particular issue has been the safe circulation of pedestrian and vehicular traffic. Reg 17 reads as follows:

'(1)   Every workplace shall be organised in such a way that pedestrians and vehicles can circulate in a safe manner.
(2)   Traffic routes in a workplace shall be suitable for persons or vehicles using them, sufficient in number, in suitable positions and of sufficient size.'

Organisations such as schools, hospitals and leisure facilities, where goods are delivered but there is a likelihood of significant numbers of pedestrians in the vicinity, need to take this provision very seriously. The requirements imply that there should be separate physical route-ways or, if that is not possible, the arrival and departure of vehicles must be managed so as to ensure that pedestrians are not exposed to risk.

There is a wide range of other measures that need to be taken to ensure safety, including signs, speed limits and safety clothing which will alert people to the risks of mingling vehicular with pedestrian traffic. All risk assessments need to address this issue fully.

**Doors, gates and windows**
These need to be constructed of safe materials and be safely managed. Regulation 14 requires:

'(1) Every window or other transparent or translucent surface in all walls or partitions and every transparent or translucent surface in a door or gate shall, where necessary for reasons of health and safety:
(a) be of a safety material.
(b) be appropriately marked.'

Amendments to the Workplace Regulations in 1995 require that *any* transparent or translucent door or barrier be made of safety glass or other safety material below shoulder height. This provision applies to any glass partitions which, if it is not made of safety glass, will present a risk to users of the premises.

In addition, windows and skylights must be capable of being opened safely (Reg 15) and of being cleaned safely (Reg 16).

Doors which slide must be able to do so without risks (Reg 18), as should other designs of doors which are power operated.

**Ventilation and temperature**

After a few hot summers and more recently some very cold winters, the temperature at workplaces has become a major issue. The traditional approach of UK law had been to prescribe a particular reading in degrees Fahrenheit. Increasingly, it has been recognised that it is the flexibility of the employing organisation which is important and that not all workplaces are comparable. The emerging legal orthodoxy is that temperatures need to be appropriate to the work being performed at a workplace and that there may be seasonal variations which need to be responded to.

The Workplace Regulations specify the following:

- Ventilation – Regulation 6
  '(1) Effective and suitable provision shall be made to ensure that every enclosed workplace is ventilated by a sufficient quantity of fresh or purified air.' (Reg 6(1))

It is clear that this requirement can be adapted to different types of workplaces. For example, in some workplaces windows are adequate to provide fresh air, in others air conditioning needs to be provided. It is suggested that air-conditioning systems be adequately maintained and reviewed so as to prevent some well-identified problems such as Legionella bacteria.

- Temperature – Regulation 7
  '(1) During working hours, the temperature in all workplaces ... shall be reasonable.'

The ACOP suggests that in normal circumstances the temperature should be at least 16°C; where work involves physical effort, 13°C. However, the key point is that there is no absolute rule; employers have to examine their own workplace and assess what the temperature should be so as to avoid risks to health and safety.

**Lighting**

The regulations here are very direct and simple:

'(1) Every workplace shall have suitable and sufficient lighting.' (Reg 8)

The intention is that the priority should be for natural light and that appropriate non-glare artificial light be provided where natural light is not possible. There are requirements for emergency lighting where loss of light would create special risks and for adequate cleaning of windows etc.

**Welfare facilities**

At the heart of much early health and safety legislation has been the requirement for basic welfare facilities at the workplace such as washing and sanitary facilities. The 1992 regulations reiterate these demands. For example, Regulation 20 requires: 'Suitable and sufficient sanitary conveniences ... at readily accessible places' and Regulation 21 requires that: 'Suitable and sufficient washing facilities including showers if required by the nature of the work or for health reasons, shall be provided at readily accessible places.'

It is assumed that washing facilities shall be 'in the immediate vicinity' and shall include 'a supply of clean hot, cold or warm water' (Reg 21(2)).

In addition, there should be 'an adequate supply of wholesome drinking water' (Reg 22) and adequate provision for clothing (Reg 21) along with adequate changing facilities (Reg 24).

**Rest facilities**

Rest facilities including eating facilities should be provided and there have to be facilities for non-smokers (it is not necessary to provide facilities for smokers). Pregnant women and nursing mothers should have facilities which are near to sanitary facilities and allow women to lie down (Reg 25).

## OCCUPIERS' LIABILITY ACT 1957

This legislation provides for compensation for victims where they are injured as a consequence of poorly maintained and managed premises.

Far more wide ranging than occupational safety laws, it requires the occupier to take 'reasonable care' to ensure that visitors to the premises are 'reasonably safe'. This legislation protects people injured on premises from hazards ranging from defective stairs and lifts to situations where someone visiting premises is attacked by animals on it.

An employee, a self-employed person using premises for work, as well as members of the public using premises in an authorised way, are all deemed to be visitors and are protected by this legislation.

The rules are discussed more fully in Chapter 5.

## WORK EQUIPMENT

Work machinery safety has always been one of the more significant areas of health and safety enforcement and practice. Work equipment is defined as 'any machine, appliance, apparatus or tool for use at work' (Provision and Use of Work Equipment Regulations 1992, Reg 2). The major risks from equipment are:

- coming into contact or being trapped between machinery and material;

- being struck by material in motion in the machinery;

- being struck by parts of the machinery being ejected;

- being struck by material ejected by the machine;

- electrocution, scalding, burns etc.

These are hazards connected with machines with moving parts. However, office equipment such as guillotines and display screen equipment also pose threats. In addition, equipment ranging from vehicles to spades and scissors can cause harm if not properly designed and its use supervised. Law in the UK has tended to concentrate on the 'classic' manufacturing machine with moving parts. The Factories Act 1961 laid down duties regarding the following:

- the duty securely to fence a machine that has moving parts;

- the duty to install an efficient stopping device in the event of an emergency;

- the duty properly to maintain guards and safety devices;

- the duty to ensure that new machinery complies with BS 5304.

Although the example on the next page concerned breach of a specific legal requirement to make equipment safe, it does not follow that the absence of specific regulation will allow an employer to escape. An electric fan positioned in a dangerous way may raise the possibility of a breach of section 2 HSWA if there is a feasible risk of harm.

SAFETY LEGISLATION – SPECIFIC DUTIES   61

---

EXAMPLE – THE CIRCULAR SAW

A 17-year-old man was working at a metal-cutting circular saw, cutting steel tubes; his woollen sweater got caught up in the machine. This caused his right arm to be dragged into the machine, he suffered severe injuries and his arm had to be amputated.

The machine had been fitted with an automatic two-piece aluminium guard which covered 300 degrees of the blade. A circlip securing parts of the guard was missing and new parts had been ordered. In fact, they had been delivered a week before the accident but the works fitter had not had time to fit them. In the meantime, the guard had been wedged with a piece of wood. The company was fined £1500, primarily because it had continued using the machine with a faulty guard contrary to s14 FA 1961.

It is worth noting that, although the prosecution drew attention to the defective guard, another obvious cause of the accident was the clothing of the employee which could easily become entangled. Employees as well as the machines themselves can create hazards! Employers must be aware of this. (*R v United Reels and Drums*, 1989)

The Offices, Shops and Railway Premises Act 1963 also requires dangerous parts of office machinery to be adequately guarded. In particular, guillotines should be guarded and items such as scissors, letter openers and knives used only for their proper purposes.

Many other pieces of equipment used at or for work can be potentially dangerous. Vehicles with defective brakes, chairs likely to collapse and electrical equipment of various sorts can pose severe risks.

REGULATION OF ELECTRICAL EQUIPMENT

Electrical installations are covered by the Electricity at Work Regulations 1989, supported by a number of British Standards.

The main demands of the Regulations are:

- Electrical systems have to be such as to prevent danger.

- Electrical systems have to be maintained so as to prevent danger.

- Every work activity involving electrical appliances shall avoid danger.

- Electrical equipment shall be suitable for use and properly maintained.

The practical implications of the Regulations include the necessity for:

- effective earthing of appliances and cutout mechanisms;

- appropriate use of guards;

- use of current breakers where appropriate;

- use of reduced voltage systems where possible.

This is supported by a safe system of wiring electrical equipment. The implications of these Regulations are that greater care should be taken in the choice of electrical equipment, its installation and use. The Regulations also apply to homes of employees where workstations are used and have particular relevance to information technology home-workers.

However, even without the 1989 Regulations, employers can be in breach of legal duties.

---

### EXAMPLE – THE LIVE BARS

Two employees were on the roof of a building throwing material into a skip. When dropping a metal sheet they caught it on the edge of live bus-bars and received severe shocks. Their employers said that they had no evidence to believe that at the time the busbars were live. The company was fined £2000 with £5000 costs. Although the case predates the 1989 Regulations and was brought under the Construction (General Provisions – Regulations 1961), the general approach is the same: never assume that electricity is safe until it has been properly tested. (*R v Smiths Builders*, 1987)

---

## LEGISLATION RELEVANT TO WORK EQUIPMENT

The Health and Safety at Work Act, the Factories Act and the Offices, Shops and Railway Premises Act continue to have relevance. However, the Provision and Use of Work Equipment Regulations 1992 are the most important. The Regulations apply to:

- all activities involving work equipment, e.g. stopping, starting, use, repair, transport, modification, maintenance, servicing and cleaning;

- all workplaces;

- employees, the self-employed and members of the public using work equipment in public places, such as launderettes.

The legislation was fully operative from 1 January 1997. There is also an amending directive from the EU which will require further provisions.

PRINCIPAL DUTIES

**Selection and provision of equipment**
The employer has to have regard to working conditions and hazards on premises and provide equipment which is constructed or adapted so as to be suitable for operations for which it is provided; and provided/used only for operations for which, and under conditions for which, it is suitable (Reg 5).

**Maintenance**
All work equipment must be 'properly maintained' (Reg 6).

**Use of equipment: creation of special risks**
Where equipment is likely to create special risks (for example, from fire, vibration, electrocution):

- 'use of the equipment must be restricted to those using it';

- repairs etc. 'must be restricted to persons specifically designated to carry out such operations ... who must have received adequate training'.

This is an important provision and aims to prevent the 'amateur' user of potentially dangerous equipment. These provisions are especially important where equipment is left on client premises by contractors or equipment is shared. Such equipment must be secured when not in use and its use closely supervised. Maintenance, including even apparently routine or obvious repairs, must only be undertaken by qualified persons. Managers must ensure that enthusiastic amateurs do not attempt to remedy problems.

**Dangerous equipment**
Equipment which has dangerous parts must:

- be designed so as to prevent worker access;

- be capable of stopping if a worker enters a danger zone, i.e. is likely to be injured (Reg 11).

These provisions, which will usually require safety guards or other protective devices to be fitted, reinforce existing UK legislation. Specifically, it should not be possible to remove the guards and maintenance should usually be possible with the guards etc. still operative.

**Other provisions**
The other major requirements are:

- to prevent risks through the ejection or fall of materials;

- to prevent risks through fire, overheating and disintegration;

- to prevent risks from explosion, liquids, gases, dust etc. (Reg 12);

- to prevent injury through excess of heat or cold in using equipment (Reg 13);

- to ensure equipment can be safely started and stopped (Regs 14–16);

- to ensure controls are safely positioned and equipment is stable (Regs 17–20).

**Information, instructions and training**
All users of equipment must be provided with suitable and 'comprehensible' information and instructions regarding the operation of the equipment and health and safety provisions. This should include how to use the equipment safely, how to deal with emergencies and problems and what to do if the equipment does not appear to be functioning properly (Reg 8).

Training must be provided in use of equipment. This is especially important for those who service or maintain equipment (Reg 9).

It is also important to note that the equipment which is provided conforms with European safety standards. The CE 'kitemark' satisfies this requirement. Managers need to check when new purchases are made that the kitemark is present.

It is also important to note that sets of specialised regulations covering equipment in particular occupations/sectors are still relevant. They include:

- Factories Act 1961;
- Abrasive Wheels Regulations 1970;
- Power Presses Regulations 1965;
- Woodworking Machines Regulations 1974;
- Agriculture Regulations 1957, 1959, 1962, 1974 (dealing with specific risks in agriculture).

The Supply of Machinery (Safety) Regulations 1992 complement the Provision and Use of Work Equipment Regulations. These require that work equipment is designed, made and supplied safely. Most equipment is covered by these Regulations which were prompted by a European directive. There is a particularly onerous requirement where equipment is potentially dangerous; here the supplier has to provide a 'technical file' which provides detailed written information on the equipment itself and its safe use and maintenance.

## DISPLAY SCREEN EQUIPMENT (DSE)

In recent years there have been a number of concerns about the impact of display screen equipment, more popularly known as visual display units (VDUs). Health problems appear to have arisen, especially musculo-skeletal problems such as repetitive strain injury (RSI), carpal tunnel syndrome and other upper limb disorders. There have also been reported problems over eye strain, skin complaints and back injury.

A European directive, No. 90/270 EC of 29 May 1990, on minimum safety and health requirements for work with display equipment led to the UK Regulations – Health and Safety (Display Screen Equipment) Regulations 1992.

It is important that these Regulations are read in conjunction with the Management of Health and Safety at Work Regulations 1992 and the Provision and Use of Work Equipment Regulations 1992.

The regulations have impact in five ways:

- provision and quality of hardware and software;

- provision of a workstation;

- the work environment in which DSE is used;

- work practices;

- management of DSE work.

However, there are some preliminary questions.

- What is DSE?: 'Any alphanumeric or graphic display screen' (Reg 1).

- What is an 'operator'?: A person 'who habitually uses display screen equipment as a significant part of his normal work'.

- A 'workstation' comprises 'display screen equipment' and 'any disk drive, telephone, modem, printer, document holder, work chair, work desk, work surface or other item peripheral to the display screen equipment and the immediate work environment around the display screen equipment'.

It is clear that the Regulations apply to the office but also the home, so long as the worker there is a 'habitual user'. The Regulations provide examples of the sort of people who are 'habitual users' such as secretary, air traffic controller, financial dealer, graphics designer, data inputter, librarian. The Regulations also suggest that some workers who use equipment are not habitual users, such as senior managers and receptionists and other groups who sometimes need to use DSE.

It is likely that any employee who uses the equipment at least 50 per cent of his or her working time will be a habitual user.

The regulations do *not* apply to:

- screens in drivers' cabs;

- screens in means of transport;

- laptop computers if not in prolonged use;

- screens for public use, e.g. at cashpoints;

- screens used for short periods, such as much scientific and medical data display;

- window display typewriters, showing only one or two lines of text.

## Principal Duties on Employers

These are:

- to carry out a 'suitable and sufficient' risk assessment of the work-station and its impact on the user.

- measures to reduce risks to the lowest reasonably practicable extent.

In practice, this means that the employer should only supply equipment which meets European quality standards and has the CE kitemark. The employer must ensure that:

- the *detail* on the screen is clear;

- the *image* on the screen is stable and does not flicker etc.;

- the screen is *adjustable* for brightness and contrast;

- the screen *swivels and tilts*;

- the screen is not subject to *glare and reflection* which cause discomfort;

- the keyboard is *tiltable* and separate from the screen;

- there is sufficient *space* around the keyboard;

- the keyboard is *not reflective, is easy to use and has clear symbols*;

- there is adequate *space* on the desk surface to use the DSE and space for comfortable use by the operator;

- if a document holder is used it is *stable and adjustable*;

- the chair is *stable and adjustable* in height and tilts;

- a *foot rest* is available.

The environment in which DSE is used should be subject to the follow-ing conditions:

- adequate *space* around the workstation;

- satisfactory *lighting*;

- control of *glare*;

- control of *noise*;

- control of *heat*;

- reduction of *radiation*;

- adequate *humidity*.

The Guidance Notes in the Regulations provide much helpful information on the safe supply and use of DSE. However, experience shows that there are other key elements of risk management for those using DSE. These cover the following.

**Eyes and eyesight** (Reg 5)
The employer is required, should the 'habitual user' request it, to provide at no cost to the user a suitable and sufficient eyesight test. Further tests should be provided at regular intervals after the initial test to ensure that there has been no dramatic deterioration.

If necessary, the employer should provide suitable 'corrective appliances' (Reg 5(5)) – normally glasses. The basic NHS glasses should be provided free, although many employers provide a range of glasses beyond that for which the employee pays.

**Training in the use of DSE**
This is not only in the use of the DSE itself, but in its safe use. The training should concentrate on awareness of the risks associated with DSE, sensible work procedures to deal with them and advice regarding how to respond to problems encountered in the use of DSE and health problems.

The employing organisation's health and safety policy (see Chapter 3) should have identified the person to whom complaints can be made and the correct procedures to follow.

## Information

All users of DSE should have adequate information on its use. This includes not only employees but other users of DSE equipment such as agency temps, work trainees and self-employed staff.

### MATERIALS USED AT WORK

Duties cover the safety aspects of materials worked on and used to work with. They can cover textiles, foods, liquids, tools, pens, pencils and the like.

The general duties on the employer are expressed as follows. So far as is reasonably practicable the employee should make:

> 'arrangements for ensuring the safety and absence of health risks in connection with the use, handling, storage and transport of articles and substances.' (HSWA s2(2)(b))

Where articles are supplied by someone else there is a similar duty on them to:

> 'ensure, so far as is reasonably practicable, that the article is so designed and constructed that it will be safe and without risk to health at all times.' (Consumer Protection Act 1987 s36)

Specific materials such as asbestos, lead and explosives are subject to specialised regulations. Thus, the Control of Asbestos at Work Regulations 1987 remain operative, as do parts of the Iron and Steel Foundries Regulations 1953, although the former will be updated because of European measures.

The Health and Safety Executive publishes a whole range of Guidance Notes on materials, such as *Safe Handling of Materials in the Printing Industry*.

The law requires proper knowledge by employers and others of the risks posed by materials and the need to prevent harm; 'doing your best' or being misinformed of risks is not adequate.

## EXAMPLES

**The toxic liquid**
A factory inspector was making a routine visit to premises when he spotted a drum of highly toxic and dangerous hydrofluoric acid. It appeared that it had got there by chance; the employers had ordered a drum of hydrochloric acid and the supplier had misheard the order and had sent hydrofluoric acid. No one noticed. An employee suffered severe burns when splashed. It seemed that no one had read the label on the drum properly.

The company was fined a total of £750. There was clearly carelessness all round regarding the ordering, storage and general management of work materials. (*R v International Radiator Services*, 1987)

**The escape of radioactive materials**
The mother of a 16-year-old girl called at a factory to check the legality of her working on telephone equipment maintenance. Her daughter was indeed working illegally. However, the investigation revealed that there was escape of radioactive materials when glass tubing broke during the removal of dials from telephones. Employees said that as many as 10 per cent of the glass tubes broke; the employers put the percentage as low as 0.5 per cent. Tests showed the employees to be correct and that, as well as the schoolgirl, several pregnant women had been exposed to very high dosages of radiation. The company was fined £5500 in all for breach of the Ionising Radiation Regulations 1958.

## HAZARDOUS SUBSTANCES

## COSHH REGULATIONS 1988 (AMENDED 1994 AND 1995)

These implement Directive 80/1107/EC on hazardous agents. They are supported by several ACOPS and apply to all workplaces. However, they have great relevance for:

- major manufacturers and bulk users of chemical substances;

- users of substances in circumstances most likely to involve high exposure levels, e.g. spraying activities;

- the so-called dusty trades, including the ceramics and refractories industries, quarrying, foundries and metal manufacturing/finishing processes;

- users of processes which generate substances hazardous to health in appreciable quantities, e.g. certain welding, cutting, grinding, milling or sieving operations;

- risks from biological agents, e.g. bacteria and carcinogens.

### Principal Duties on Employers

These are to:

- make health risk assessments;

- control exposures;

- carry out monitoring;

- arrange for health surveillance, in particular:

  - health examinations;
  - environmental monitoring;
  - the maintenance of control measures, e.g. exhaust ventilation systems.

A 'substance' is defined as 'any natural or artificial substance, whether solid, liquid, gas or vapour, and includes human pathogens'. Lead and asbestos are specifically excluded from the Regulations.

A 'substance hazardous to health' includes:

- a substance with a prescribed or approved occupational exposure limit, as listed in HSE Guidance Note EH/40 *Occupational exposure limits*;

- a substance in the Approved List under the Chemicals (Hazardous: Information for Supply) Regulations 1994;

- human pathogens;

- any dust in substantial quantities in air;

- *any other substance arising from work which may be hazardous to health.*

The rolling procedure is as follows:

1. *To assess the risk* presented by substances to the health of employees
   and others. This can be done by making a list of all substances, identifying points of use, and carrying out risk-assessment procedures, if
   necessary through the use of experts.

2. *To control exposure to substances.* This is done by preventing exposure
   or, if this is not possible, by adequate control. So far as possible control should be achieved other than by provision of protective equipment such as masks for employees. Measures which are relevant here
   include improved ventilation, substitution of less hazardous substances, reduced number of employees exposed, improved facilities
   for washing etc.

3. *To maintain, examine and test control measures.* This requires testing of
   respiratory equipment, ventilation etc. Careful records of examinations and reports should be kept.

4. *To monitor exposure* through the use of valid occupational hygiene
   techniques, especially where maximum exposure levels (MEL)
   apply.

5. *To carry out health surveillance* of employees exposed to risk; medical
   records should be available and employers must respond to specialist medical advice about risks to health. There will always be a need
   to keep individual records.

6. *To provide training* for employees regarding both the nature of the risk
   and the precautions to be taken. Information also has to be provided
   for others who carry out work which has risks.

### APPLICATION OF COSHH TO DEAL WITH CARCINOGENS AND BIOLOGICAL AGENTS

Amended Regulations and ACOPS were published in 1995 to reflect
fully directives dealing with carcinogens and biological agents.

The schedules to the Regulations contain the key information regarding which substances and agents are prohibited from use or are subject
to specific limitations. Included in carcinogens are mustard gas, arsenic,

coal tar and chromate. Biological agents are classified into four categories. These are:

1. Unlikely to cause disease.
2. Can cause disease but there are effective treatments.
3. Can cause disease but there are effective treatments: it may spread to the community.
4. Causes severe disease and can spread and there is usually no effective treatment available.

Included are bacteria, micro-organisms and viruses etc., especially affecting those working with animals. The ACOP sets out procedures to be adopted so as to avoid harm. Risk assessments need not be made for category 1, but must be for 3 and 4. The preventive measures comply with the general strategy of health and safety law, i.e. prevention is the first priority and protective equipment a last resort.

## NOISE

### NOISE AT WORK REGULATIONS 1989

This implements Directive 88/188 EC, which is currently under review. More rigorous standards are expected.
   The Regulations require action at three noise levels:

- 85 dB (A)
- 90 dB (A) daily level
- 200 Pa of impact noise

The major duties on employers are as follows:

- to reduce risk to the lowest level reasonably practicable;

- to undertake 'noise assessments' if the noise is likely to be above 85 dB(A);

- if noise is above 90 dB it must be reduced other than by ear protectors – between 85 and 90 dB employees can ask for ear protectors;

- where noise is above 90 dB the area should be designated an 'ear protection zone' and be clearly marked and monitored;

- ear protection equipment is properly maintained and properly used;

- employers have to provide information, training etc.;

- employees have a duty to use protective equipment if the noise level is above 90 dB and to report problems 'forthwith'.

All noise assessments are to be made by competent persons; it is advisable to retain records of noise assessments. Employers need to introduce a noise-control programme to identify sources of noise, establish priorities etc.

## VIBRATION

This includes use of pneumatic drills through to use of DSE. It is likely that new provisions will be introduced to implement a European directive.

## CONSTRUCTION WORK

The Construction (Design and Management) Regulations 1994 implement the European Temporary and Mobile Construction Sites Directive 1992. It was recognised that the construction industry was characterised by:

- high accident rates;

- a high incidence of casual/self-employed people;

- the complexity of many construction projects;

- often poor levels of training, skills etc.;

- frequent weak management.

The basic legal strategy of the directive was consistent with other European health and safety law, i.e.:

- It emphasises management's role.

- It emphasises risk assessment and appropriate preventive measures.

- It looks for effective planning and coordination.

- It expects all activities to have safety built in.

The regulations require safety to be built in to all construction designs and work. Most projects require a safety plan to be drawn up and a safety file kept. They also require an individual to oversee the work (usually where contractors are used it is the client), called the planning supervisor. Their responsibilities include the following.

- Draw up, or cause to be drawn up, a safety and health plan setting out the rules applicable to the construction site concerned. This plan must also include specific measures concerning (particularly dangerous) work.

- Prepare a file appropriate to the characteristics of the project containing relevant safety and health information about the materials and maintenance required.

- Set out arrangements for the project which take account of the risks to health and safety during its operation.

The plan must cover the time scale, the contractors, the contract phases etc. It must also detail the liaison arrangements, control access to the site, possibly qualifications of staff, safety standards, use of equipment etc.

The language of the Regulations regarding the nature of the safety plan (and safety file) are relatively narrow. The duties are confined to construction and to workers. However, ideally the safety plan should reflect the impact of work on other non-construction/maintenance staff.

It appears sensible when devising the plan and the file to:

- note their different roles. The plan is a strategic document which will also fulfil the demands of cooperation and coordination from Regs 9 and 10 of MHSW regulations 1992. The plan will ensure, so far as is reasonably practicable, the health and safety of all persons at work by virtue of the project; the file helps the occupier of premises to ensure proper repair and maintenance to avoid later risks to health and safety.

- include appropriate arrangements for:
  - the management of construction work, and
  - monitoring compliance by all persons.

The safety file is prepared 'in respect of each structure comprised in the project and contains any information included with the design ... and any other information which it is reasonably foreseeable will be necessary to ensure the health and safety of any person carrying out construction on or in the structure at the time; and ... [the construction company should] ensure that on completion ... the file ... is delivered to the client.' As set out above, this aims to ensure that the client is aware of materials, maintenance/repair requirements etc.

## WHEN SHOULD THE PLAN BE DEVISED?

The plan should be prepared as early as possible, not least because there will be cost implications and a need to allow adequate time for discussion, training, compliance with procedures etc. Much of the burden falls on the client – this needs to be reflected in the specification and in tender prices. At this stage the plan will be in draft form but it should be used:

- for costing;

- as a means of assessing the competence of those tendering regarding health and safety standards;

- as part of the planning phase more generally; and part of the overall risk-assessment process.

The task will probably involve answering at least the following questions:

- What are the description and likely length of the project?

- What health and safety risks are there to workers? How will they be minimised?

- When should the work ideally be done – weekends etc.?

- What information is required on all aspects (materials, vehicles etc.) of the project?

- How many workers are likely to be involved?

- How much disruption will there be?

- What activities present particular risks?

- How much vehicular traffic will there be?

- Will materials be stored? If so, where? Will they be accessible?

- What services/facilities will workers need access to?

## PRINCIPAL TASKS FROM THE REGULATIONS

- To check what activities are covered – what is 'construction work'? The definition of construction is wide. The law is not confined to large development/construction work but includes smaller-scale work. The 'non-exhaustive list' of activities from the relevant European directive includes (see Regulations):

    - conversion and fitting out
    - renovation
    - repairs, upkeep
    - painting and cleaning.

- To appoint a planning supervisor from a range of competent persons; to select a competent contractor.

- To notify the HSE about the work, if required – if the work is likely to involve at least 30 days' work or 500 person hours.

- For the planning supervisor to devise the safety plan and safety file and ensure health and safety.

- To ensure that adequate resources are available to the project.

## HANDLING LOADS

Along with the use of DSE, legislation has identified manual handling as an activity exposing workers to risks, especially of back problems and work-related upper limb disorder (WULD). Back pain and injuries account for millions of lost working days across Europe. The Manual Handling Regulations 1992 apply the usual legal strategy to this activity. This is:

• Assessment of risk if manual handling is in operation.

• Exploration of whether handling can be eliminated.

• If not, can it be automated or mechanised?

• If not, measures such as information, training and advice should be applied to minimise risk.

## PERSONAL PROTECTIVE EQUIPMENT (PPE)

Helmets, spats, boots, gloves, goggles, harnesses, ear protectors and boilersuits are examples of some of the most widely used equipment to protect employees from some work risks.

The Personal Protective Equipment at Work Regulations 1992 have formalised this area of health and safety law in accordance with a European directive on the same topic.

PPE is defined as:

'all equipment (including clothing affording protection against the weather) which is intended to be worn or held by a person at work and which protects him against one or more risks to his health or safety.'

The Regulations do not apply to equipment in sport, transport (e.g. seat belts) or to work situations already subject to special regulations such as Noise at Work Regulations 1989, Control of Asbestos Regulations 1987 and COSHH Regulations 1988.

### PRINCIPAL DUTIES (REG 4)

• Suitable and effective equipment shall be provided except where risks have been controlled by other more effective means.

- Self-employed people shall use PPE except where controlled by other more effective means. This approach exemplifies the **'last resort'** approach of law to PPE (see below), i.e. goggles or helmets should only be provided if all other options to deal with risks have been explored and not found to be feasible. Examples of where other methods might be feasible include fixed screens rather than eye protectors, or mechanical transportation of heavy materials removing the need for gloves and reinforced shoes or boots.

- Equipment should be provided free for the user.

- The equipment must fit the user and, if necessary, be adapted to the individual.

In addition, before equipment is provided the employer must undertake a risk assessment to ensure that the proposed PPE is suitable (Reg 6). The employer must ensure that the equipment is in an efficient state and in 'good repair' (Reg 7). There should also be storage facilities when PPE is not in use (Reg 8) and employees must be provided with 'information, instruction and training' in the use of PPE (Reg 9).

The other major duties are that the employer has to take reasonable steps to ensure that PPE is properly used by employees and that every employee uses the equipment in accordance with training and instruction (Reg 10).

These Regulations are in line with the approach and basic demands of all modern safety legislation. They require the employer to start from a position whereby it is possible to carry out work without PPE. For example, if there is dust in the atmosphere the first question must be whether it is possible to use equipment or a process which prevents dust getting into the atmosphere. If this is not possible, improvements to air extraction and ventilation must be explored and consideration given to change in working hours and even building design. Only when all the possible options have been pursued should masks or the like be used. The masks must be suitable for the job and for individual employees. They may need to be provided in different sizes and special ones supplied for those with respiratory problems, asthma etc. The mask should not make working more difficult or create new risks by, for example, making it more difficult to see when working.

The equipment provided should conform with the European (CE) kitemark and be maintained and upgraded when necessary.

## HAZARD PREVENTION AND RESPONSE

The EU Framework Directive made explicit the requirement for all employers to provide protection from 'serious and imminent danger'. The Management of Health and Safety Regulations 1992, Regulation 7, require:

- 'establishment of procedures to be followed in the event of serious and imminent danger';

- nomination of 'competent persons' to implement 'evacuation from premises' such as fire wardens, first aiders;

- adequate 'health and safety instruction' to deal with danger;

- provision for persons at work 'to stop work' and 'immediately proceed to a place of safety'.

As considered in Chapter 3, the entitlement of individuals to stop work is backed up by the Employment Rights Act 1996, which protects employees who stop work from being 'victimised' such as by being dismissed, suspended or otherwise disciplined. The only defence for an employer who takes such action is to establish that the staff had been properly instructed in emergency or danger procedures and had behaved unreasonably.

It is important that the evacuation procedures take into account any special groups such as those with disabilities, the young and non-employees. Premises should have clear signs, and health and safety policy documents should include information on responding to danger. It is also important to note that, although fire, gas leaks, explosions and the like are the eventualities which the law has mostly in mind, danger can also come from faulty equipment and from dangerous people. Workers in the financial services sector are frequently subject to attacks, hold-ups and even kidnapping. The 'danger' procedures need to deal with these risks.

In dealing effectively with danger, employers must:

- identify and assess risks, especially from fire, substances and including risks from dangerous human beings;

- ensure that premises are adequately designed and protected and have adequate escape and/or safety procedures;

- provide clear written information and signs so people can be safe;

- provide alarms and other equipment to alert people to dangers, including intruder alarms;

- ensure adequate training in dealing with likely problems and competent staff for emergencies.

## SAFETY SIGNS

The occupiers of buildings are required to use the correct signs regarding exits and the like in the event of fire. However, there are other requirements for adequate labelling, in particular the Chemicals (Hazard Information for Supply) Regulations 1994. The main signs are set out in Figures 4.1 and 4.2.

It is important to note that signs are colour coded. The colours are as follows:

| | |
|---|---|
| Yellow | Hazard |
| Red | Prohibition |
| Blue | Recommendation to be safe, e.g. to wear hard hat |
| Green | Escape/safety procedures, e.g. for fire |

Employers and occupiers of premises have general duties to employees and others to take reasonable steps to make premises reasonably safe. These arise under section 2(2)(a) HSWA and section 2(2)(a) of the Occupiers' Liability Act 1957. Adequate signposting and warning of risks are covered. Therefore, defective lifts, slippery floors, broken windows and loose handles on doors, all waiting to be fixed, should at least be warned of.

Warnings have to be such as to enable the person using the premises to be reasonably safe. Notices simply stating 'Danger' or "Work in progress' or even 'Out of order' may not be adequate as they do not identify the precise nature of the risk. Warnings must also offer the visitor to, or user of, premises a viable option; requiring people to jump over holes in floors or climb a very steep slope because steps are broken would create new risks. The occupier of premises would not escape liability if there was an accident in those situations.

Figure 4.1: Prohibitory signs

No smoking

Smoking and naked flames forbidden

No access for pedestrians

Do not extinguish with water

Not drinkable

No access for unauthorised persons

No access for industrial vehicles

Do not touch

Safety signs should always:

- clearly identify the hazard;

- make plain how the reader can avoid or minimise risk;

- allow for the characteristics of the group of people affected – age, language abilities etc.

*Figure 4.2*: Hazard warning signs

The law takes the view that putting up notices does not of itself relieve the occupier from responsibility; it simply helps to indicate that some steps have been taken.

## WORKING TIME

Until recently, the UK had little or no legislation relating to working hours aside from limitations applying to specific occupations such as airline pilots and lorry drivers. Research evidence indicates that long, unbroken working hours are the cause of accidents, errors and illness, especially stress-related disorders. The problem is compounded if long hours are combined with monotonous work or work subject to high pressure levels.

All other states in the EU have established legislation or binding collective agreements limiting working hours and requiring weekly and yearly breaks. In November 1993 the EU adopted the Working Time Directive after considerable debate and controversy. Strictly, the directive should be termed the non-working directive as it specifies the need for breaks (rest) from work. 'Working time' is defined as a time during which the worker is 'at the disposal of the employer'. This includes time travelling between sites or on business, but not to and from the normal workplace and home. It may include time spent on stand-by, emergency cover etc.

The key provisions, implemented in the UK on 23 November 1996, are:

- an uninterrupted break of 11 hours in 24 hours;

- a weekly break of 35 consecutive hours, averaged over 14 days, in principle to include Sundays;

- a maximum working week of 48 hours, averaged over 4 months, unless the worker has genuinely consented to longer hours or collective agreements have developed particular practices;

- to require that any shift of 6 hours or more has an adequate break;

- that night shifts should not normally exceed 8 hours. 'Night' means a 7-hour period to include 12 midnight to 5 am. Working 3 hours in this period makes the worker a night worker who must then receive annual health checks;

- a paid annual holiday of at least 4 weeks which should not be 'bought out'.

The directive provides many 'derogations', i.e. industries and occupations such as postal, agricultural, emergency services and residential and care facilities which are subject to surges in demand or a need for constant service delivery. However, it should be noted that a derogation is not an exemption. Employers still need to ensure adequate breaks, arranged so as to prevent health problems. In any event, MHWR apply and require employers to provide protection from work risks, including fatigue and stress.

The directive, which applies at least to the public sector even if the UK government does not introduce new laws. It requires the following:

- a need to have data on working hours by staff, including managerial and professional staff;

- provision of rest facilities to allow breaks from workstations;

- work planning to keep within the legal framework;

- particular attention to arrangements and facilities for night workers;

- budgeting for paid holidays;

- policies to maximise the use of work time;

- careful management of self-directed staff, homeworkers and those who travel a great deal.

## EMPLOYING SPECIAL GROUPS OF STAFF

### YOUNG WORKERS

A European directive in 1994 established health and safety standards for workers under 19 years of age. UK legislation, such as the Employment of Children Act 1973, has long imposed limits on work for those under compulsory school age. In addition, specific legislation had laid down rules for safe use of machinery or prohibition from particular work activities such as working with lead or cleaning machines. The Health and Safety (Young Persons) Regulations 1996:

- provide for shifts of usually no more than 8 hours;

- restrict work to the daytime;

- require allocation of work and its management so as not to put too much strain on young people;

- provide adequate medical surveillance.

## PREGNANT WOMEN AND NURSING MOTHERS

In 1994 MHSWR was amended to incorporate the health and safety provisions of the European Pregnant Worker directive. The directive requires adequate protection for pregnant women and for those who have recently given birth or are breast feeding.

The strategy is a familiar one. Reg 13A of MHSWR requires employers of women of child-bearing age to do the following:

- include in risk assessments risks particular to pregnant women and those who have recently given birth;

- be aware of those particular risks. Guidance Notes from the HSE (*New and Expectant Mothers at Work*) specify these. They include lifting, excess heat and cold and exposure to specified substances such as mercury;

- redeploy a pregnant woman etc. on full pay if she is exposed to such risks and her present work situation cannot be made safe;

- redeploy her from night to day work if medical evidence is that she should not be employed at night;

- suspend the woman on full pay if redeployment is not possible.

The provisions only come into effect after the woman has notified her employer that she is pregnant or has recently given birth. A breach of the employer's duties where injury is caused entitles a woman to sue for damages for breach of statutory duty; the employer can also be prosecuted.

# 5

# *The Common Law and Health and Safety*

Previous chapters have considered the nature and impact of safety statutes and regulations which are enforced by fines and the use of Improvement and Prohibition Notices. These can be imposed regardless of whether an accident or injury has occurred. However, safety law also has mechanisms to provide compensation or other remedies for people who have suffered losses as a result of poor safety standards at work. Employees may have been killed, injured or have contracted an occupational disease. They might have been attacked, harassed or have endured unhealthy or extremely unpleasant working conditions which their employer appeared consistently to ignore. They may have lost their job for protesting about, for example, an allegedly dangerous vehicle, fumes, lax maintenance standards or for refusing to work with violent patients/clients or the like. These issues will now be considered.

## RELEVANT AREAS OF LAW

The major areas of law which provide redress for individuals are:

- Law of negligence
- Occupiers' Liability Acts 1957 and 1984
- Breach of statutory duty
- Law of contracts of employment.

These impose liability and award compensation by applying different approaches and rules; in most workplace situations all have relevance.

## THE LAW OF NEGLIGENCE

Legal principles applicable to the work environment have been developed by judges over many years. They are evolving continuously and can respond to new situations and new hazards. Recent examples of the law of negligence applying to new issues are:

- successful claims for stress-related illnesses;

- successful claims for illnesses associated with 'passive smoking';

- compensation for individuals involved in major disasters such as the King's Cross fire;

- compensation for people living near to factories producing asbestos who suffer asbestos-related illnesses.

The law of negligence has the ability to respond to current and emerging concerns, going way beyond traditional claims for compensation following occupational accidents and illnesses. Details of some of the cases are set out later in the chapter.

The law tends not to change rapidly but nonetheless this area of law is dynamic. It should be noted that there is often considerable tension in the process of legal developments. Judges express anxieties about 'floodgates' opening if all new issues are responded to. Courts want clear evidence of harm – physical or psychological. They expect medical evidence, especially where harm is psychological of a 'recognisable psychiatric disorder'. Clinical depression requiring medication and/or therapy is now recognised but courts generally expect a technical 'label'. For conditions where injury is physical, proof of harm is usually straightforward.

The law of negligence asks two basic questions:

- Is the injured person someone the employer ought to have reasonably foreseen as likely to be injured if work was not managed carefully?

- Did the employer reach the standard of care which the reasonably competent employer would have done in the circumstances?

If the first question is answered 'yes' and the second 'no', this will, in principle, entitle the victim (plaintiff) to claim that there was a breach of the law of negligence and that compensation (damages) is due.

Clearly, an employer can potentially be liable for a far wider range of people than simply employees. For example, perhaps it should have been anticipated that a badly maintained machine or a failure to respond to an emergency such as a gas leak might affect not only employees but subcontractors' employees, agency temps, visiting sales staff and even members of the public on or off the premises. The scope of the law of negligence is extremely wide and is *not* dependent on a contractual relationship, be it of employment or of some other nature. The only limitation on liability is the presence of someone you could not have foreseen, for example a trespasser or burglar. A particular issue is the duty owed to those who respond to emergencies such as the police and doctors. Unless these 'rescuers' behave in a foolhardy way, they are usually able to make a claim if the employer's carelessness created the emergency.

---

### EXAMPLE – THE CHIP SHOP FIRE

Due to carelessness a fire occurred in a fish and chip shop and quickly spread to the whole building. The fire brigade was called. Above the shop was a flat in which it was thought the tenant might be. A fireman went into the flat and was suffocated. A successful claim was made against the proprietor of the fish and chip shop. It made no difference that the victim was a professional 'rescuer'. (*Salmon v Seafarer Restaurant Ltd*, 1983)

---

### REASONABLE FORESIGHT AND VULNERABLE WORKERS

One of the most important and controversial aspects of the law of negligence concerns the liability of the employer to those who are already in some way vulnerable. This might be because they have disabilities, are asthmatic, pregnant or have a psychiatric condition.

The legal questions are whether the employer owes a duty of care at all to such people and if so, of what nature? If the employer actually knows of the vulnerability, then it can *actually* foresee that harm might be caused to, say, an asthmatic if he or she works in a smoky atmosphere. Similarly, if a woman tells her employer that she is pregnant, the employer should foresee that asking the woman, say, to carry heavy loads or work in a hot, stuffy environment is likely to harm her or the unborn child. In such situations not only will a duty of care usually be owed but the amount of damages awarded will reflect the plaintiff's vulnerability. This is called the 'egg-shell skull' principle, a rule most popularly known as 'you take your victim as you find them!'

What if the employer is not aware of the vulnerability? Generally speaking, the law requires you only to foresee harm to normally 'robust' people, i.e. those of normal susceptibility. If an individual working in an office with fairly low noise levels becomes suddenly deaf due to a rare pre-existing problem with his or her ears, the law will not require you to have 'reasonably foreseen' such an eventuality. Problems have often arisen in applying these rules to people involved in traumatic events. (See also Chapter 6 regarding the wider agenda.)

---

### EXAMPLE – THE FORTH BRIDGE DISASTER

Workmen were painting the bridge. It became extremely windy and materials were being blown around. A large metal sheet was placed on the back of an open truck and in order to anchor it and prevent it causing damage one of the workers sat on it. The truck was followed by another vehicle containing the plaintiffs.

There was a violent gust of wind. This blew the sheet and the workman off the truck. The workman was blown off the bridge and died. The incident was seen clearly by the plaintiffs. They both suffered depression, nightmares and their family life was devastated.

Their claim in negligence was rejected. The court decided that the defendants who employed them could not be expected reasonably to foresee that an accident which did not directly involve them, where the deceased was not related to them and whom they could not help or rescue, would cause such psychological damage. The judge commented that people at work must expect to put up with such incidents – their reaction was, in effect, extreme and unpredictable!

The case has been criticised, not least because the men had worked together for a considerable time. (*Robertson v Forth Bridge Co*, 1995)

## Reasonable care

The plaintiff has to prove that the employer failed to take reasonable care, i.e. fell below the standard reasonably to be expected. Whether reasonable care was taken will probably depend on two issues:

- Identification of level and nature of risk.

- Identification of how the reasonably competent employer would have responded to the risk.

Obviously, the greater the risk the greater the care demanded. Storage of very hazardous substances requires considerable precautions; a very remote risk requires fewer precautions. Employers, in the words of one judge, are required to guard against 'reasonable probabilities not fantastic possibilities'. However, employers are assumed to be well informed about the risks attached to substances and equipment. Once again, the law will not condone ignorance or 'turning a blind eye'.

---

### Example – the slippery floor

Due to very severe storms a factory in the north-west of England was flooded. The flooding caused oil and grease from machines to make the factory floor very slippery. The factory owner put sawdust on the floor and instructed employees to be careful. An employee slipped on the floor and was badly injured. He claimed that the factory owner had failed to take reasonable care; the floor was so dangerous that the factory should not have been used. The court did not agree. It considered that, although the risk existed, it was not so serious as to require the employer to close down the factory with all the economic consequences for the employer and employees. The precautions taken were a reasonable response. (*Latimer v AEC Ltd*, 1952)

---

## The role of risk assessments

It should be noted that the argument that safety is too expensive or too hard to achieve will not be accepted easily by courts today; certainly it will never be accepted where risks are great. Courts are reflecting increasing concerns about occupational accidents and ill-health, and are seeking to raise standards through their imposition of high awards of damages. Although almost invariably employers will be insured against claims, court actions can cause severe adverse publicity for an organisation.

As explained in Chapters 3 and 4, the statutory framework requires employers to undertake the following tasks in relation to all likely workplace hazards:

- Assess and record the risks they create for employees and others.

- In the light of the assessment, undertake appropriate preventive measures, i.e. minimise the risk.

- Monitor, review and respond to changing work situations.

These legal duties have direct and crucial relevance for the law of negligence. Risk assessments should not only have identified the nature and level of risk(s) but also who is at risk. The severity of risk will have been recorded. Risk assessments determine the steps which need to be taken to minimise risks. This will usually require employers to consider a range of options. If the risk is caused by a noisy workplace, the options explored should start with those which would eliminate risk and only finally move to providing ear protectors.

This strategy is exactly the same as is required by the law of negligence. Risk assessments require the techniques of 'reasonable foresight' of harm. 'Preventive measures' are only a similar way of expressing 'reasonable care' required of employers by the law of negligence.

The position is, therefore, remarkably simple. An employer who has satisfactorily complied with the statutory obligation to undertake and appropriately respond to risk assessment will almost certainly have taken 'reasonable care'. Claims in negligence will therefore fail. On the other hand if, following an accident, the HSE successfully prosecutes an employer for, say, breach of the Noise at Work Regulations, a claim in negligence will be likely to succeed.

The areas of law are, of course, not fully compatible. They have different objectives and different strategies. Nonetheless, there is a clear affinity between the questions posed by both, and the legal messages are clear.

## SCOPE OF THE LAW OF NEGLIGENCE

As discussed earlier, negligence has a wide scope; duties can extend to non-employees and members of the public. But what if employees work off the premises, at home or are under the direction of someone else, for example because they are hired out or seconded? One thing the law does not say is 'out of sight, out of mind'. The employer still has to take adequate precautions, provide adequate training and offer proper support. Window cleaners, for example, have been injured while working on badly maintained or dangerous buildings under the control of someone else. Employers can still be negligent if they fail to provide proper instructions or equipment. Even if employees work overseas or are subject to supervision by someone else, there is still the possibility of a successful claim in negligence.

The lessons of the case below should not be lost. Employers need to satisfy themselves before arrangements are agreed that the third party has good safety standards and that supervision and work procedures are effective.

---

### EXAMPLE – THE CRUSHED SEAMAN

A seaman was the employee of a UK company but hired out to a Dutch company. He suffered a severe accident while in the Netherlands working on a tug in Rotterdam harbour. One of his duties was to untie the tug when directed to by the tug's skipper. The instruction was a tap on the window of the tug. On the day in question (the weather was atrocious) he failed to hear the tap, the tug moved away from the jetty and he was thrown into the water. He was badly crushed between the tug and jetty.

He claimed in negligence against his employers (although he could also have claimed against the Dutch company). His employers argued that they could not have failed to take 'reasonable care' for his safety as they had no effective means of supervising his work. The argument was rejected. Employers still have to take reasonable care of employees. Specifically, where their employees are under the direction of someone else they still have to satisfy themselves that work practices and safety management are appropriate. (*McDermid v Nash Dredging and Reclamation Co Ltd*, 1987)

---

However, as a recent case has shown, the employer does not have to guard against all risks. For example, it was not necessary to inform an employee who was to work in Ethiopia of the advisability of taking out insurance to guard against financial loss if caused by others. In this case, his car was damaged in a collision with an inadequately insured Ethiopian national (*Reid v Rush and Tompkins Group plc*, 1990). The law sees a distinction between the need to take reasonable care and provision of blanket protection which is not necessary.

## SOME RECENT EXAMPLES OF CASES IN NEGLIGENCE

### Asbestos dust in the neighbourhood

The number of deaths caused by asbestos has recently been estimated as being likely to be over 100,000 by the year 2020. Currently, around 3000 people die from asbestos-related cancers and other illnesses. Mostly they are workers from the construction industry. However, in this case, the victims were not workers but people who in their childhood had played in the proximity of a factory manufacturing asbestos.

It was decided that, even though scientific knowledge at the time the plaintiffs inhaled the asbestos dust (in the 1950s) was limited, it was sufficient to require the factory owners reasonably to have foreseen that if they failed to control the dust harm would be caused. This would include harm to non-employees. It should be noted that the defendants in this case had paid out over £300 million in damages in the period 1986–96. (*Hancock and Margerson v Turner and Newell*, 1996)

### Fall from a ladder

Mr Davies was working on an upstairs window using a twelve-foot ladder. A sudden gust of wind blew him off the ladder and as a result of the fall he was unable to work again and was in constant pain.

The negligence of the employers was in failing to train him in how to deal with problems when working at a height and how to secure his ladder safely. (*Davis v Chester-le-Street Council*, 1995)

### Compensation for brain damage

The plaintiff, who worked for the Ministry of Defence at Gosport, Hampshire as a civilian worker, was exposed to five times the legal limit of methyl ethyl ketone (MEK) while stripping missile warheads. He retired on health grounds in 1986, the exposure having caused him to be unable to speak properly and to lack physical coordination.

MEK is used as a solvent as a substitute for white spirit. The negligence here was in failing to monitor exposure levels being aware of the risks. It was accepted that 'allowing the plaintiff to be exposed to five times the recommended level was negligent'. The plaintiff received £280,000 compensation. (*Bradshaw v Ministry of Defence*, 1996)

### £211 for laboratory animal asthma victims

Four laboratory technicians obtained damages after contracting animal asthma while working at Glasgow University. Their job was to feed and water animals including rabbits, rats and guinea pigs. The reason they became ill was because their employer had failed to provide appropriate protective equipment. Specifically, there was a failure to provide adequate masks, protective clothing and gloves.

In addition, there were insufficient health checks and failure to explore options for cleaning out the animals which would have eliminated the risk of contamination to humans. The technicians were also not provided with adequate training. (*McKay and others v University of Glasgow*, 1995)

## Negligence – what if caused by your own employee?

The other side of the coin in the law of negligence is where, for example, reckless driving or careless operation of a machine inflicts harm on someone else. This might be on a fellow employee or someone totally unconnected with the workplace. The Employer's Liability (Compulsory Insurance) Act 1969 requires employers to insure against injury or loss caused to their employees.

There is also the principle of **vicarious liability** whereby if the negligence causing an accident or incident took place in the 'course of employment' the employer will have to pay compensation to an injured person. Only if the employee 'was on a frolic of his own' at the relevant time, for example using a work machine for entirely personal purposes, or, as a delivery driver, deviating off a route to see a friend, will the employer escape liability.

---

### Two examples

**The explosion in the petrol station**
A petrol tanker delivery driver was delivering to a petrol station. Contrary to strict instructions he lit a cigarette, threw down a match and caused a massive explosion. It was decided that the employer was vicariously liable; the employee was still doing his job, albeit in an unauthorised way. (*Century Insurance Co Ltd v N Ireland Transport Board*, 1942)

**Crushed by the milk float**
A milk delivery driver was instructed never to carry passengers on his milk float. He did so, and when carelessly turning a corner he injured a young boy who was helping him deliver milk. The boy's foot was crushed between the float and the kerb. Despite persistent warnings the employer was held vicariously liable; the driver was still delivering milk! (*Rose v Plenty*, 1976)

---

## Breaches of discipline

If at the time of the accident the employee was acting contrary to instructions, what is the effect? Case law suggests that it is most unlikely that employers will escape liability.

Even if the negligence took place when the employee was working under the direction of someone else, for example on secondment, the employer will still generally be responsible for the consequences.

## Occupiers' liability

It has already been seen in Chapter 4 that HSWA and other statutes, but especially the Workplace Health, Safety and Welfare Regulations 1992, establish rules and standards for work premises. However, the Occupiers' Liability Act 1957 (OLA) also establishes principles of liability on 'occupiers' to take reasonable steps to ensure that premises are 'reasonably safe' when being used by visitors. If not, and injury occurs, the visitor can sue the occupier for compensation.

If, therefore, an employee, consultant, agency temp or, indeed, a member of the public lawfully on the premises falls over on a dangerous and slippery floor or trips on a broken stair or is electrocuted by live electric wires strewn about, claims can be made. Whether they will be successful depends on the plaintiff(s) establishing that all the demands of the regulations have been met. Some key definitions for these purposes are:

- **Occupiers** – an organisation or people who have a degree of control over premises; includes owners and tenants and some subcontractors, especially working long term and on greenfield sites.

- **Control** – implies the ability to regulate entrance to and use of premises.

- **Visitors** – includes everyone lawfully using premises, employees, self-employed people, workers for third parties such as agencies and subcontractors and members of the public.

- **Premises** – includes moveable (e.g. transport and work equipment) and immoveable structures. This has special relevance to lifts, stairs, floors, obstructions and adequate lighting, warning of hazards, and equipment and procedures for emergencies such as fire.

- **Reasonably safe** – taking such precautions by way of maintenance, repair and supervision as would the reasonably competent occupier in the circumstances (s2 (2) OLA).

### Some special situations

The law imposes liability on occupiers if an injury is caused to a visitor when that visitor is using premises in an ordinary way. The law requires visitors to take reasonable care for themselves, for example by avoiding obvious hazards and following instructions. The standard of care owed by occupiers clearly varies according to the risks inherent in premises and the extent and nature of use by visitors. Busy places such as railway stations, department stores and leisure/sports centres must maintain high standards because of particular hazards, volume of use and numbers of people unfamiliar or less familiar with risks and emergency procedures.

However, workplaces are sometimes used by people who are more conscious of hazards and risks. The law reflects this in section 2(3)(b) OLA by allowing an occupier to rely on the fact that people using premises in connection with their 'calling' (i.e. craft, occupation) will guard against risks 'ordinarily incidental to it'. Obvious examples are window cleaners, emergency and maintenance personnel, but the law in no way expects such people to eliminate or cope with all risks themselves.

---

### EXAMPLE – MENDING A LIFT

An employee of a firm of maintenance engineers visited a company's premises to repair a lift, a task he had carried out before. The lift machinery was in a machine house on the roof. On previous visits he had noted and reported to the occupier that the doors to the machine house were broken but they had not been mended. On the present occasion the doors had been jammed open; he assumed they were safe. They were not, and when he put his weight on them they collapsed and he was badly injured as he fell.

The occupiers were held liable. Although the employee knew something of the hazards of getting to the lift machine house, he did not appreciate the additional risks caused by the jammed doors. The premises were

---

Conversely, premises used by children have to have higher standards applied to them, because the law expects that children are less likely to appreciate risks and less likely to be careful (section 2(3)(a) OLA).

What if signs are erected warning of hazards? As discussed earlier, the law says to do so does not exonerate an occupier; the signs etc. have to enable visitors to be reasonably safe. Signs which simply state 'Danger', 'Men working, 'Take care' are generally inadequate. They must be specific and offer visitors viable options to avoid injury (section 2(4)(a) OLA).

The major area for disputes has been where an occupier uses or has used a subcontractor for work of 'maintenance, construction or repair' and an accident occurs which, it is claimed, is directly linked to that fact.

The work may have been badly done (roof repairers may have been used but tiles still fall off and injure a visitor), the work itself may create different hazards (electric cables strewn about corridors cause an employee or visitor to trip over) or new hazards caused (a contractor may interfere with power supplies causing employees in an office block to be electrocuted).

Clearly, in many of these situations the contractors themselves can be sued in negligence where their carelessness has caused injury. However, occupiers who use such subcontractors may nonetheless also be liable if they have not selected a competent contractor or overseen work adequately and managed the premises properly at the relevant time (section 2(4)(b) OLA).

These duties must now be read in the light of changes in practice required by both the Management of Health and Safety at Work Regulations 1992 (MHSWR) and the Construction Design and Management Regulations 1994 (CDM).

Risk assessments and the development of effective safety plans and procedures are at their heart. Applied to the use of subcontractors, the position appears to be as follows:

- Using contractors creates particular risks. A potential contractor unable to carry out a proper risk assessment is unlikely to be considered 'competent' for the purposes of OLA. Additionally, the contractor should provide safety policies, accident records, insurance details and an adequate safety plan for the work in order to be seen as competent.

- Regulations 9 and 10 MHSWR require adequate 'cooperation and co-ordination' of the work. This implies that effective communication, liaison and monitoring should take place. This will then meet the requirement in OLA that the occupiers should check that work by contractors 'is properly done'.

- The development of safety plans and safety files under CDM will also ensure that occupiers using contractors will have taken steps to ensure that work is properly done and that reasonable steps have been taken to make the visitor reasonably safe when using premises.

OCCUPIERS' LIABILITY – SOME GENERAL GUIDELINES

- Employers must have adequate information on who uses their premises, for what purposes and with what frequency.

- Risk assessments should be carried out.

- Premises must be maintained properly and managed so as to make them safe for all users.

- Information and warnings must be comprehensive and sufficient for the full range of users, and adapted, if necessary, where there are special users such as children, the disabled and the public.

- Contractual negotiations with subcontractors must establish clear work procedures, communication systems and defined areas of responsibility. The health and safety implications of subcontractors working on premises must be clearly thought through.

- Adequate insurance cover must be obtained by all and there must be no assumption that responsibility for premises can easily be passed to others.

## ACTIONS FOR BREACH OF STATUTORY DUTY (BSD)

Statutory duties regulate the workplace; employees and others are sometimes injured when a statute is broken. For example, where dangerous substances are stored insecurely and there is an explosion or leak causing injury; where a machine is inadequately fenced and an employee working at it is cut severely; where employees are working at a height on a building site with no safety harnesses or helmets being provided, and one is injured by falling to the ground.

Although the Factories Act 1961, the Offices, Shops and Railway Premises Act 1963 and other safety statutes have as their primary aim the effective regulation of the workplace, they can also provide a means of compensation where individuals are injured.

The more modern regulations, for example most of the 'Six Pack', can also generate compensation claims. The law asks a series of precise questions to decide whether compensation is payable to a victim by the person who had the duty imposed on them. This is a very exact area of law; it has none of the generalities of the law of negligence. If the answer to all the following question is 'yes', the employer will be liable.

- *Was the duty to comply with the statute imposed on the employer?* Or was it one which was primarily imposed on, for example, an importer, supplier, retailer, or on someone to whom the employer had lawfully delegated it?

- *Was the 'victim' the one that the statute was designed to protect?* A statute designed to protect employees may not protect a visitor to a factory who is injured through the failure properly to inspect, maintain or operate a working machine. For example, a marketing consultant visiting factory premises would generally not be able to obtain compensation for BSD if he or she tripped and fell into an inadequately fenced machine, contrary to section 14 Factories Act 1961.

- *Was the accident or injury sustained in a way that the statute was designed to prevent?* Safety statutes and regulations have generally been designed to counteract a specific injury. Sometimes accidents occur in a less predictable way. For example, regulations affecting tunnelling may require the roof to be secured so that it does not fall on employees below. If an employee operating an earth-moving vehicle collides with some roofing material which has fallen to the tunnel floor and which causes the vehicle to roll over, injuring the driver, will the injured employee be able to sue? Yes, but only if the court is willing to view the statute as having a general objective of preventing accidents in tunnels, not just roof falls causing injury to heads.

- *Did the breach of duty actually cause the injury?* It may be that although the employer broke a statutory duty the actual accident was caused by somebody else; not least, that the injured person themselves was totally to blame through flouting safety statutes. This is unlikely, but nonetheless a victim still has to prove the causal link. If both employer and employee contributed to the accident, courts can apportion liability.

## TWO EXAMPLES

**Skin infection**
A lathe operator who had worked for a company for 26 years contracted dermatitis. The employers had warned of the risk of skin infections and had issued barrier creams. They claimed he was adequately protected. However, there was evidence that they had also 'haphazardously and inefficiently' cleaned the machine, contrary to section 29 Factories Act 1961. This was the major cause of the dermatitis and the employee obtained compensation. (*Yates v Rockwell Graphic Systems*, 1988)

**Molten metal**
A man was injured while working in metal production. Molten metal splashed on his feet and caused severe burning. Spats were provided at the factory but employees did not like wearing them, although the employers strongly advised them to do so. The employers successfully defended a claim for breach of statutory duty since they had discharged their obligation to provide safety equipment. The employee had failed in his duty to 'wear' it.

However, the injured employee did succeed in a claim for compensation in negligence; the lax standards regarding safety and safety equipment generally indicated a lack of reasonableness in providing a safe workplace. (*Bux v Slough Metals Ltd*, 1974)

## IMPACT OF BREACH OF STATUTORY DUTY

Most safety statutes and regulations have the potential to allow an injured person to claim for compensation. Liability is imposed according to the very precise wording and purposes of the statute. Judges generally have the ability to give as wide or narrow an interpretation of statutes as possible. Increased regulation implies increased potential for claims, and the COSHH Regulations are of great significance for occupational diseases and disorders.

The need to expand the UK's regulatory framework because of directives from Europe adds a further dimension. It should also be noted that British judges, when interpreting and applying UK legislation which has been passed to implement European law, are adopting a more 'purposive' approach to their task. This means that they are placing greater emphasis on the purpose the law was trying to achieve rather than simply seeking the dictionary definition of a word or phrase. Thus, amendments to UK law which are derived from directives to improve health and welfare as well as safety standards might well lead judges to the enforcement of a wider and more proactive role for employers. It is likely that law relating to compensation for accidents etc. caused by breaches of safety laws will be greatly changed in the next few years and provide increased protection for victims of health problems as well as accidents.

## HEALTH, SAFETY AND THE CONTRACT OF EMPLOYMENT

This is an emerging and increasingly important area of law. Because it is also developed by courts and tribunals it can adapt to new issues and new priorities. Health and safety issues usually arise in this area in three ways:

- Claims by employees that employers have broken the employment contract by failing to provide a safe workplace or support over health and safety concerns. This can amount to constructive dismissal.

- Claims that an employee was unfairly or wrongfully dismissed for refusing to obey an order which the employee thought was dangerous or that would expose him or her to risks to health.

- Where an employee suffers a 'detriment' for stopping work or advising others to do so in response to 'imminent danger'.

Cases are heard in industrial tribunals but sometimes employees claim in County Courts or in the High Court for damages. There is, of course, no need for an employee actually to have been physically injured; the law is simply concerned with a contract being broken.

### PRINCIPLES OF LAW

Contracts of employment contain implied obligations as well as express ones, such as terms relating to pay and hours of work. Implied obligations arise by judges establishing through case law certain base obligations on the part of both employer and employee. There are three key areas of relevance to health and safety:

- *The obligation on the employer to provide a safe workplace.* The detail of the implied obligation is obtained from HSWA, MHSWR and any other general or specific regulations.

- *The obligation of an employer to provide 'trust and support'.* This is a wide-ranging obligation to investigate complaints or anxieties about hazards, to try to find a solution and to be sympathetic to employees' concerns generally. The employee has an equivalent obligation. Here it is likely to imply the need to warn of health hazards and to cooperate with safety procedures and training. This reinforces Reg 13 MHSWR.

- *The obligation on an employee to obey lawful orders.* Disputes can arise where the employee has safety anxieties and, say, refuses to carry on working but is then dismissed for misconduct.

Until fairly recently it was difficult for employees to win such cases, but now the law has shown more support for them.

---

### Two examples

**The goggles**
A long-serving female employee worked as a welder. She was provided with goggles according to recommended safety procedures. She wore bifocal glasses which made wearing the goggles difficult and caused her headaches. She understood that goggles were available which would have been better for her eyes and wrote to her employer about her problem. Her letters were ignored for eight months. She left her job claiming that her employer was in breach of the implied obligation to provide support. This was so serious as to have undermined the whole contract, and she considered she had been constructively dismissed. Her claim for unfair dismissal was successful. (*BAC Ltd v Austin*, 1978)

**Fear of mugging**
A recently employed young female employee had as part of her job the duty to take cash to the bank. Local newspapers had reported a series of muggings of pedestrians in the area. She stated that she did not want to take cash to the bank alone because of the danger. Her employer ignored her worries. She, too, claimed she had been constructively dismissed and won. The employers had failed to support her. (*Keys v Shoe Fayre Ltd*, 1978)

---

In both of the examples above employers were presented with real anxieties regarding safety, and in both cases they could and should have explored options. In the first case, better goggles might well have been obtained or, failing that, Mrs Austin's work rearranged. At the very least the employer should have responded to letters and discussed the issue with her.

In the second case, the employer should have thought about safer ways of getting cash to the bank. Perhaps two employees could have gone or a security firm employed? Offering training in karate would probably not have sufficed! It was certainly inadequate to put the responsibility on the employee.

## REFUSAL TO WORK

Disputes frequently arise over assertions by employees that, for example, an oil rig or a tunnel is unsafe, a building too old, or their work involves high levels of violence from bus passengers, pub customers or psychiatric patients. Employers will sometimes consider that the danger has been exaggerated or the allegations are really masking an industrial dispute or claim for higher pay. They may sack employees for disobeying their orders. Employees may then claim for unfair dismissal and test the validity of the employer's argument.

It is never easy to apply the law in circumstances where employees consider that there is a risk to their health, but if the employer's reaction is that the risk is slight or the employees are over-reacting or simply troublesome, this can lead to legal problems. The EU Framework Directive 1989 required legislation to ensure that:

'Workers who, in the event of serious, imminent and unavoidable danger, leave their workstation ... may not be placed at any disadvantage because of their action and must be protected against any harmful and unjustified consequences.'

This was implemented in the UK via the Employment Rights Act 1996. This establishes that a worker who is dismissed or otherwise suffers detriment for stopping work or refusing to undertake specific tasks where he or she believed there was imminent danger is entitled to compensation for unfair dismissal or compensation generally. In unfair dismissal claims such dismissals are automatically unfair; i.e. they cannot normally be defended and there is no qualifying period (usually two years) for claims.

The legislation protects most self-employed workers as well as employees. However, if an employer can show that the behaviour of the worker(s) in question was unreasonable in the light of their knowledge and training, claims might not succeed. In effect, therefore, if the employer has effective safety policies and practices, especially regarding danger, and can demonstrate that workers had open to them options other than simply stopping work when faced with problems, industrial tribunals may support the employer.

# 6

# *The Wider Agenda*

In recent years a number of health and safety issues have come into prominence which have not traditionally been within the scope of the topic. Sometimes these issues have arisen because of the changing composition of the workforce, especially the increased number of women; sometimes they have evolved through equal opportunities policies; sometimes because of growing awareness of health and welfare matters generally. Additionally, the changing ways in which people are working – increased shift and night work and, in many sectors, longer, more concentrated periods at work, as well as more people working at or from home – have pushed the boundaries of health and safety law even further.

This chapter is concerned with the application of legal rules and standards to some of these newer issues. These issues include:

- smoking and smoking policies;
- alcohol abuse and alcohol policies;
- drug abuse and policies;
- violence against staff and violence policy development;
- sexual harassment, bullying etc.;
- AIDS policies;
- policies to respond to the mentally and physically disabled at work;
- protection of pregnant women and nursing mothers;
- stress.

Many of these have been the subject of inquiries and/or Guidance Notes and booklets by the Health and Safety Executive.

There is no single reason for these issues having come to the fore or for their having a health and safety dimension. Clearly some, although not all, are linked. Smoking, violence and sexual harassment often pose dangers to the health and bodily security of employees, no less than do dangerous machines or substances. Hence, the employer may well need to provide an effective response, in part to comply with the legal framework of health and safety. Specifically, they are covered by the Management of Health and Safety at Work Regulations 1992 and are matters which risk assessments should have identified and for which adequate preventive measures should have evolved.

This chapter deals with a selection of these issues by illustrating how the basic legal rules set out in Chapters 3–5 apply in practice.

## SMOKING

It is clear that most employers now have some form of smoking policy at work and that many are now updating or reviewing their policies.

The law has long seen smoking as a work hazard in particular situations, especially risk of fire or explosion. Examples are:

- Explosives Act 1975
- Gas Safety (Installations and Use) Regulations 1984
- Control of Lead at Work Regulations 1980
- Road Traffic (Carriage of Dangerous Substances in Road Tankers and Tank Containers) Regulations 1992

### LEGISLATION

Section 2 of the Health and Safety at Work Act 1974 established a duty on an employer to ensure the health, safety and welfare of all employees (s2(1)), including the working environment (s2(2)) 'so far as is reasonably practicable'. Most prosecutions for health or safety have recently been made under section 2. As yet there has been no successful prosecution for failing to have an effective smoking policy to protect health and welfare, but the potential for prosecution is clearly there. It is also important to note that Section 7 imposes a duty on employees to take reasonable care at work for the safety of themselves and others. 'Others' in principle can include those affected by smoking. An employer is perfectly justified in reminding employees of their statutory duty.

## Control of Substances Hazardous to Health Regulations 1988 (COSHH)

The (COSHH) Regulations, effective since 1990, do not specifically identify cigarette smoke as a hazardous substance, although there are circumstances where it can be if combined with other substances. However, although the safety inspectorate remains non-committal on whether the COSHH Regulations are relevant to smoking, the question is potentially subject to prosecution and/or enforcement notices under the 1974 Act and other more recent legislation.

## Management of Health and Safety at Work Regulations and Workplace Regulations 1992

Relevant demands are as follows:

- Employers have to undertake and provide a written risk assessment for all employees and for others. Risks to health caused by tobacco need to be part of that assessment, especially for 'high risk' groups such as pregnant women and vulnerable groups such as asthmatics.

- Employers need to minimise identified risks by taking preventive measures. These could include effective ventilation/air-conditioning policies, but a smoking policy could be introduced more cheaply and effectively. **The law expects employers to remove the source of risks rather than to ameliorate the consequences.** It is crucial that risks from tobacco smoke which emanate from beyond employees are taken on board. Included here are customers, clients, agency staff and contractors who smoke. The simple legal principle is that the greater the risk the greater the care that needs to be taken. Preventive measures can include limiting exposure to tobacco from, say, drinkers in a pub by changing working hours as well as improving ventilation; ideally, a smoking policy should be developed.

- Employees need to be more actively consulted and involved in health and safety matters and their views sought on health and safety concerns. This is not an 'optional extra' but an intrinsic part of the legal structure. Do employees want a policy?

- By virtue of the Workplace Regulations, since 1 January 1996 workplaces must have rest facilities for non-smokers. Rest facilities include canteens, lounges, reception areas etc. Unless an employer wants to have 'dual' facilities, the logic is to introduce a smoke-free policy in these areas. It remains to be seen whether a smoking area in, say, an open canteen will be adequate to protect non-smokers.

## The law of negligence

It has recently been decided in UK law, albeit as a result of out-of-court settlements (confirming decisions in other parts of the world), that in some circumstances failure to respond to the harmful effects of smoking can amount to negligence by an employer. This occurs if:

- the employee's health suffers, i.e. he or she requires medical care; and the medical evidence supports the contention that health has, indeed, suffered as a consequence of passive smoking; and

- the employer should have reasonably foreseen that an employee (or other person) might suffer harm as a consequence of smoking. The medical evidence is mounting now for employers to be expected to foresee harm; and

- the employer failed to take reasonable steps to guard against the risks. This means that it failed to take such measures that a reasonably competent, comparable employer would have done. The reasonable steps clearly include a smoking policy and perhaps other environmental measures.

*Bland v Stockport BC* (1992) is an important example. Here a local government employee, a keen amateur singer, suffered respiratory infections due to the smoking of colleagues combined with inadequate ventilation and general building design. Despite considerable dispute as to the importance of this settlement, the message has got through to managers that there are considerable legal risks in failing to respond to smoking at work.

This approach mirrors successful claims in negligence in other parts of the world; for example, *Wilks v American Tobacco Co* (1993) and *Scholeun v Dept of Health* (1993) in Australia. To date in the UK, there has been no reported case in negligence where compensation has been awarded by a court (as opposed to an out-of-court settlement).

The law of negligence also has relevance when non-employees are affected. It can apply to make an employer vicariously liable for loss and damage caused by smoking by employees. This applies regardless of whether smoking was banned or not, so long as the smoking was 'in the course of employment'.

The leading case on this issue is of long standing. A petroleum delivery driver, subject to and reminded of a disciplinary rule which forbade smoking while working, smoked while watching petrol from his tanker fill tanks at a service station. He threw down a match which caused an explosion, destroying adjacent premises.

In a negligence claim against the employer the defence that smoking was well known by employees to be contrary to rules was ineffective. The law's view is that so long as the damage was caused while work was in progress the employer is liable. The only rearguard action for employers to reduce the likelihood of claims is effectively to monitor and rigorously enforce disciplinary rules to prevent smoking (*Century Insurance v Northern Ireland Transport Board* , 1942).

### The contract of employment

The employer is subject to the implied obligations to provide a safe workplace and at least to provide trust and support when dealing with complaints by non-smokers.

## DEALING WITH SMOKING

Before turning to the lawful introduction of a policy, and the nature and impact of relevant legal rules prescribing the legal parameters, it is worth bearing in mind the basic contractual rules which can be applied to any newly employed staff. It is lawful to:

- select only non-smokers and/or to limit applications to non-smokers or to select only those prepared to comply with your policy. There are no civil liberties or anti-discrimination legal rules of any relevance whatsoever;

- make a total or limited ban on smoking at the workplace or even off premises a specific term of contract. It is, however, vital to ensure that new staff have seen the policy and agreed to it forming a part of their contractual rules;

- reserve the right in the contract to extend limitations on smoking at some future date or to otherwise make amendments;

- make smoking a matter of staff discipline, and to determine which category of misconduct it is in;

- make smoking a specific issue in pre-employment health screening.

The law gives employers very wide discretion in all of these matters. What is essential is that information is provided *before* the contract of employment is agreed to.

As regards non-employees, such as freelance staff, consultants, contractor's staff, agency staff and visitors to the premises, the legal rules are equally simple. A smoking policy can form a part of the contractual or non-contractual licence on which they enter premises. In other words, an employer using an agency for temporary staff can limit the temps they are sent to those prepared to cooperate with the smoking policy. Members of the public can be told by notice or leaflet that the workplace is non-smoking and that if they infringe the rule they will be asked to leave. Where the workplace is an aeroplane in flight or a ship on the high seas this is clearly problematic! However, most people accept the reasons for the message and do cooperate.

Despite these basic legal rights it is, of course, advisable to give notice of change, time to adapt and generally to provide sympathetic management of the change.

### Introducing new rules for smoking
For existing staff where a policy is being developed the legal situation is more complex, but in practice has given rise to relatively little case law and few disputes.

Because of the way in which legal rules operate, it is vital to consider carefully answers to the following questions at an early stage in policy development:

- Will there be a policy document?

- If yes, how will it be used, to whom will it be provided and with what purpose?

- What are the range and content of the document itself? What style of language will it adopt? Specifically, will it deal with the big question – what happens if someone breaks the policy?

- Is it intended that the document be regularly reviewed and revised?

- If there is no formal policy document, how will the policy be implemented?

- Most importantly, what is the current nature of employee contract documentation? Are employees provided with written and signed employment contracts or simply a written statement of terms?

- What are the current disciplinary rules applying to staff?

- Does the contract documentation provide for contract variation and development or does change have to be agreed to?

On the assumption of a formal policy document and an intention to make the policy effective (which the law increasingly requires, see above) thorough disciplinary rules following the legal basics should be adequate.

### Legal rules on variation of contract terms

If the existing written material is silent on smoking and the employer wishes to introduce a policy or ban, this will constitute a variation in contract terms unless the contract makes provision for unilateral change by the employer. Otherwise changes have to be agreed by the employees. Technically a collective agreement, i.e. where the policy is agreed with unions, will not suffice of itself to make the change lawfully. The notice of a new policy/ban will constitute an offer by the employer to vary contract terms which the employee is able to accept or refuse. Acceptance can be done formally (e.g. by signifying consent in writing) or can be deemed from conduct after the passage of a period of time without objection. There is no specific time scale for this, although custom and practice suggest that if an employee carries on working and does not object the change will have been lawfully carried out after 2–3 months. It is vital to note that the mere fact that a staff questionnaire reveals, say, 85 per cent in favour does not, of itself, alter this basic legal situation – the employment contract is an individual contractual relationship and has to be dealt with accordingly.

### Formal non-smoking policies – their effect

- A policy will not, of itself, change contract terms unless agreed to as set out above.

- It should be decided whether a written policy has employment contractual status. If so, it must be effectively incorporated in the individual's contract, following the above rules, and the language of the policy must be appropriate.

This implies that employees must be aware of the policy and its status and, ideally, have personal copies. The policy must then have an approach, e.g. in terms of disciplinary rules applying to smoking, which is consistent with the organisation's disciplinary code.

It must be appreciated that there is a key legal difference between material which is descriptive and that which is prescriptive. A policy should not, therefore, speak in language which 'hopes' or 'expects' employees to comply with the policy when the disciplinary code states that smoking is grounds for 'instant dismissal'!

### Refusal to comply with the change

While most employees go along with a change, a problem can arise over refusal by one or two. Enforcing an 'unagreed-to' ban can amount to constructive dismissal. It may, nevertheless, be a fair dismissal for 'some other substantial reason' (under the Employment Rights Act 1996). If, for example, there are good reasons for the ban, adequate notice, consultation and a sympathetic approach to those who find it hard to give up smoking, a tribunal may well find it fair. However, even if there are grounds to dismiss, e.g. health factors and employee pressure, the employer must still handle the dismissal fairly. The following cases are illustrative.

A company, following the advice of the local Health and Safety Inspectorate, issued a newsletter indicating an intention to introduce a no-smoking policy. Departmental meetings were held and in August 1987 notice was given of a ban from January 1988. This was held to be reasonable and made the dismissal fair of an employee who refused to go along with it. He had had sufficient time to adapt. (*Rogers v Wicks and Wilson Ltd*, 1988)

Mrs Watson, a smoker, had worked for a company for several years. A ban was introduced while she was on sick leave. She was told to stop smoking or be dismissed when she returned. This was held to be an unfair dismissal as it was handled insensitively with no consultation and no consideration of options which may have been open to the company. (*Watson v Cooke, Webb and Holton*, 1988)

Mrs Dryden smoked 30 cigarettes a day. Until 1991 her employer set aside a smoking area so that she could smoke during working hours. This was withdrawn and she claimed constructive dismissal. In the Employment Appeal Tribunal it was stated:

'Where a rule is introduced for a legitimate purpose, the fact that it bears hardly on a particular employee does not, in our view, in itself justify an inference that the employer acted in such a way as to repudiate the contract.' (*Dryden v Greater Glasgow Health Board*, 1992)

The practical points which emerge from these basic legal rules are clear and emphasise the need for a well-prepared and sensitively introduced policy. Law has rarely challenged an employer's motives for a policy and has never been persuaded that, for example, stressful jobs require a freedom to smoke. However, law is increasingly emphasising the 'how' part of change, especially the need for consultation.

The basic messages from law are as follows:

- Be absolutely clear on what you want to achieve, who is affected, the consequences of breaking a policy and whether flexibility for development is required.

- Ensure adequate and effective consultation, even where the employment contract authorises change. Sudden announcements and draconian penalties for smoking will not be effective in law and might cause employees to claim that trust and confidence have been broken.

- Ensure that everyone is consulted, especially those on leave.

- Check the style and language of all documents.

- Allow time for change.

- Provide support for those experiencing problems.

**Dealing with problems**
Usually problems can be dealt with by operating disciplinary rules. The normal unfair dismissal case law applies where an employee is dismissed for contravening a policy. The legal outcome will depend on individual facts including whether there was awareness of the ban/policy; evidence of warnings and rigorous adherence to disciplinary procedures; consistent reaction to other breaches; opportunities for the employee to make a case that there were exonerating facts, e.g. family bereavement; previous conduct record of the employee.

# ALCOHOL

Alcohol can clearly affect performance and can expose others and employees themselves to risk of injury. In principle, it is a risk which should be assessed and has several parallels with smoking, as in some occupations and workplaces the risks associated with even relatively small amounts of alcohol can be great. Similarly, if an employee affected by alcohol causes an accident the employer may be vicariously liable. The evidence is that even small intakes of alcohol impair judgement and performance and considerably increase workplace risks. Where work involves operating machinery, driving etc., alcohol can be a major issue which has to be addressed.

Alcohol may also be a contributory factor in:

- violence
- harassment
- bullying.

Where an employer wishes to introduce a policy limiting or prohibiting alcohol consumption on premises or during working hours or at other times, the legal rules applicable to the introduction of a smoking policy will apply. Employees, therefore, need to be consulted on a policy in most cases, but new staff can have provisions included in their contracts. Similarly, breaches should be handled fairly, including disciplinary rules.

It is *essential* that rules are applied in a even-handed way. In *Dairy Produce Packers Ltd v Beverstock* (1991) the claimant was dismissed for drinking in a public house during working hours. He complained that three other employees had been caught when drunk: all had been warned but not dismissed. The employer argued that the claimant's case was more serious because he worked away from the factory and was in a position of trust. There were, however, no clauses in the contract dealing with alcohol.

The dismissal was held to be unfair. There were no grounds for seeing that drinking outside the factory was more serious. If it was meant to be, the disciplinary rules should have spelt that out.

Dismissal for alcohol abuse, i.e. dependency, rather than for being drunk/disorderly/violent etc., is usually considered part of the legal rules relating to 'capability' dismissals. The general principles set out in *East Lindsey District Council v Daubney* (1977) should be applied. These include:

- full investigation of the facts, especially the employee's medical condition;

- full consultation with the employee;

- opportunities for second opinions;

- consideration of possible options aside from dismissal.

## Drug abuse

In addition to the risks associated with alcohol, such as causing an accident to a fellow worker or third party, some drugs are illegal substances and the employer as well as the employee may well be liable under the Abuse of Drugs Act 1971. It is essential, therefore, that employees do not have possession of, trade in or use classified drugs at work.

Screening can be used in various ways, including:

- pre-employment testing of applicants;

- testing all or part of the workforce at set intervals or on a random basis;

- testing a particular individual who has been involved in an accident or dangerous occurrence;

- when drug abuse is suspected for other reasons;

- as part of a rehabilitation programme.

The agreement of the workforce to the principle of screening/testing should be obtained; the written consent of the individual must also be obtained in each case. Medical confidentiality must be assured: managers may be told only whether an employee is considered fit or unfit for work.

Pre-employment testing is the easiest form of screening to introduce as all job applicants can be informed at an early stage that they will be required to submit to screening; those who are unhappy about this are free to withdraw and seek employment elsewhere. Testing existing employees may be more difficult to introduce, other than for particular jobs or after an accident. The procedure for counselling people whose tests are positive will need to be carefully thought through in advance. Individuals must be informed of the consequences of a positive test result before testing takes place.

It is now possible to detect the presence of some drugs in small samples of body fluids or urine. Tests are available that can detect opiates, cocaine, barbiturates, amphetamine, cannabis and LSD in urine. Special procedures are necessary for collecting samples (ensuring that they cannot be tampered with and are actually provided by the person being screened), arranging testing and confirmatory testing, and for follow-up action if a screening sample proves positive. Screening can therefore be quite costly for the employer. It can most easily be introduced by organisations that already have occupational health facilities and carry out regular medical examinations of existing staff or new entrants.

There are a number of problem areas. Test results need careful validation and interpretation as both false positives and false negatives can occur. Individuals who know that they will be screened on a particular day may be able to avoid taking drugs for a sufficient period beforehand to ensure a negative result. It is particularly important to choose a laboratory equipped to do the initial immuno-assay screen followed by confirmation of positives by gas chromatography/mass spectrometry techniques.

Screening itself will never be a complete answer to the problem of drug abuse and its results must always be supplemented by a professional assessment of the employee. The policy to screen will require audit on a regular basis (at least every two years) to ensure its continued relevance and smooth working. Effective screening procedures are required to support disciplinary action, especially summary dismissal.

## WIDER POLICY DEVELOPMENT

There is a great deal of advice available on policy development. The following is a suggested approach to a drug abuse policy.

### The essentials of a policy

Because every workplace is different, employers need to develop a policy tailored to the size, structure and nature of their business and also consider other relevant factors. In general, a successful policy will be based broadly on a written statement which will do the following:

- state that the purpose of the policy is to ensure that the possible consequences of drug abuse on the individual, other employees, the public and the environment are avoided or reduced to a minimum;

- state that the policy applies to everyone in the organisation;

- define drug abuse;

- state the organisation's concern for safety and the environment, and for the health and well-being of employees;

- explain that abuse could lead to a health problem, including addiction, and that there is a need to identify abusers and to intervene and provide the necessary help quickly;

- confirm confidentiality of any discussions, especially regarding drug dependency;

- make clear that absence for treatment and rehabilitation will be regarded as normal sickness absence and that confidentiality will be maintained where addiction is involved;

- recognise that relapses may occur;

- state that the employer will try to ensure that an employee returns to the same job after treatment or, where this is not advisable, try to provide suitable alternative employment;

- explain that if help is refused and/or impaired performance continues, disciplinary action is likely to follow;

- explain that dismissal may be appropriate in cases of gross misconduct;

- provide for an induction and ongoing education programme about the dangers of drug abuse;

- provide for the policy to be monitored and reviewed regularly.

**Policy management**
Good policy management will:

- ensure that the policy forms an integral part of the company's overall policy on health and welfare matters;

- delegate responsibility for developing and implementing the policy to a named person of senior rank in the company. In larger companies this may be a personnel officer or occupational health specialist; smaller companies may wish to obtain advice from local community services. The Health and Safety Executive's Employment Medical Advisory Service may be able to advise on what is available;

- seek the commitment of line managers and employees to the policy by fully consulting workplace representatives, including any safety representatives appointed under the Safety Representatives and Safety Committees Regulations 1977 and Health and Safety (Consultation with Employees) Regulations 1996, at all stages of developing the policy;

- provide training for everyone concerned with health, safety and industrial relations issues at work, including trade union representatives, before its introduction. Training should include a general course on the issues of drug abuse, the signs to look for, how to deal with staff at risk or who seek help and where to refer them for professional advice;

- encourage employees with drug/alcohol problems, through an education programme, to seek help and treatment voluntarily;

- consider applying the company's disciplinary procedure to employees who refuse help, particularly if the safety of other employees is jeopardised, or unacceptable behaviour and poor standards of work persist;

- include in the disciplinary procedure features such as warnings, a reasonable time for improvement and the right to appeal against disciplinary action;

- ensure that the disciplinary procedure has been fully observed before considering the possibility of dismissal;

- agree with workforce representatives what action to take where an employee:

  - admits to needing help
  - is found abusing drugs
  - is found trafficking in drugs
  - has a relapse after receiving treatment.

## AIDS

During the 1980s there was a great deal of debate and some controversy, including case law, on some of the issues surrounding the impact of Acquired Immuno Deficiency Syndrome (AIDS). There have also been misconception and prejudice. Clearly, AIDS is both serious and currently incurable. The law has been concerned to identify the health and safety issues and to ensure that those with AIDS do not suffer unfair treatment at the workplace.

Medical advice suggests that some, although very few, occupations are unsuitable for sufferers from AIDS; possibly some food-handling and some medical-care occupations. To allow an employee with AIDS to continue working in such circumstances may put an employer in breach of various health and safety duties. If, however, the employer dismisses the employee, case law suggests that this can amount to unfair dismissal. The employer ought to consider alternative work and, if other employees have been putting on pressure, explain to them clearly the level of risk and proposed response; the employer should not simply react by instant dismissal.

This is clearly a complex and sensitive issue. Expert advice is readily available, as are organisations able to offer training and counselling. The key thing is to be well informed.

## VIOLENCE

Violence covers fighting, threats and intimidating behaviour more generally. It can occur in various circumstances:

- *Violence by another employee.* This could be through fighting or threat of it. The injury could be inflicted intentionally or carelessly, more probably the former. It can take place on or off premises and within or outside working hours.

- *Violence by a non-employee but someone who is a part of the working environment.* This could include a patient, client, customer, traveller, pupil at school, taxpayer, benefit seeker etc.

- *Violence by a complete outsider.* This could include a burglar or other type of apparent criminal using violent and threatening behaviour.

It should be borne in mind that violence and threats are also, potentially, the concern of the police and the criminal justice system. The crimes involved might range from attempted murder, manslaughter, grievous bodily harm through to common assault and threatening behaviour.

An employer may have legal responsibility to victims of violence or the threat of it as a consequence of MHSWR 1992, whereby violence is an assessable work risk and the employer has failed to introduce preventive measures such as physical protection, training and enforcement of disciplinary rules. There is a considerable amount of guidance and advice from HSE and others on violence at work and employers need to familiarise themselves with this and respond appropriately.

## CASE STUDY: COMBATING VIOLENCE AND SECURITY RISKS ON A UNIVERSITY CAMPUS

University X is a multi-campus higher education institution with over 16,000 students, many of whom are mature or female. Some teaching and support staff, along with the students, are located on campuses in urban centres, generally with easy access to members of the public or, indeed, intruders. Some parts of the campus have legal rights of way crossing them. Buildings are generally small, with many entrances. There are staff and student car parks adjacent to all buildings and there is the usual range of leisure, welfare and sports facilities.

Following the so-called Six Pack of new regulations in 1992, the university appointed a health and safety officer. There were well-established health and safety committees. The new health and safety officer introduced risk assessments and deployed questionnaires to identify what staff and students saw as the major health and safety hazards on campus.

The results were unexpected. Violence or the fear of it and a general sense of vulnerability emerged as key issues. There were reports of intruders, thefts, threats and attacks, and the police often became involved. There were some security measures and staff in place, but they were used primarily to protect the premises and equipment.

During the summer of 1995 the university appointed further senior personnel with health and safety remits (although these were not their sole concern). They participated in the health and safety committees and became aware of the anxieties over violence and security. However, they were also aware of resource constraints, along with the ethos of a university which is to encourage open access and a lack of formality.

The university's governing body recognised that steps had to be taken, but that investment in this area, especially in hardware and buildings, had to be appropriate and effective.

A strategy was developed which was fully implemented by the summer of 1996. The major challenge was to change the culture of the university, especially causing staff to be more aware of risks and more prepared to alter behaviour. The in-house newsletter featured security issues prominently. A 'lock it or lose it' campaign was launched, but this ran into some opposition. Staff resented having to lock doors, saying: 'It's not my job to do it' or 'Students should be welcomed and not have to wait outside locked doors'.

The security manager responded by saying: 'We are about to invest serious money in security measures but it will be money poorly spent if staff do not play their role by taking the most basic steps to prevent theft.'

Security cameras have been installed but, of course, require personnel to monitor them so as to prevent attacks etc. Lighting has been improved and dark corners minimised.

Most importantly, the university improved its accident and incident reporting systems, placing an emphasis on incidents. Between January and March 1996 there were 36 incidents, including assaults on staff, assaults on students, theft and damage to property, intruders and other incidents.

Clear messages were given out about, for example, what 'acting suspiciously' is. The message was that if staff or students have doubts, 'report it'.

A further decision was to end the practice of contracting out for security, as 'the ability to train our own people in the very specialised role of campus security will lead to improved personal safety on all sites'.

In the short term, there was an apparent rise in the number of incidents; this was explained by higher levels of awareness. Important, too, was the incentive to report with the expectation that something would be done. During this period staff, in particular, felt that at last their fears were being taken seriously and there was a discernable improvement in morale.

## Stress at work

Over half the people who are identified by research studies as suffering from the symptoms of stress report that their stress is work related. In some occupations, for example psychiatric nursing and teaching, the proportion of people with work-related stress can rise to three-quarters or more. The symptoms of stress can range from headaches to heart attacks to increasing dependence on alcohol and drugs. Figure 6.1 sets this out diagramatically. The base of the triangle indicates the higher numbers of people with, generally, non-life-threatening problems; the apex the few who will die from occupational stress.

Research has shown that there is a strong correlation between work conditions and stress. Examples are:

- excessive noise
- excessive dust
- poor lighting
- overcrowding
- shift work and unsocial hours
- violence and social isolation.

However, the widely accepted definition of the underlying cause of stress is the inability of an individual to meet the demands which work puts them under. It is becoming increasingly recognised that the culture

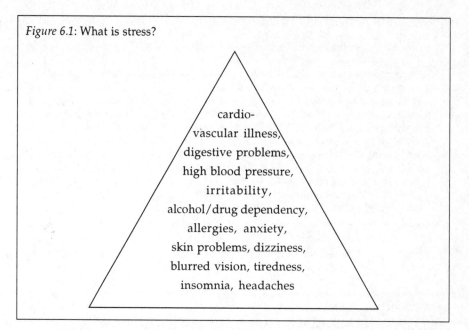

Figure 6.1: What is stress?

cardio-
vascular illness,
digestive problems,
high blood pressure,
irritability,
alcohol/drug dependency,
allergies, anxiety,
skin problems, dizziness,
blurred vision, tiredness,
insomnia, headaches

of organisations is a prime cause of stress, for example the expectation of long hours or that lunches are taken at the employee's desk, or where an unwillingness to take on extra duties or extra work is seen as a sign of weakness or lack of commitment to the organisation.

There are also indications that the introduction of new technology, especially DSE, can increase stress levels. In this regard the Health and Safety (Display Screen Equipment) Regulations 1992 should ensure some improvement, despite being primarily geared towards the prevention of physical disorders.

A number of the other factors likely to cause stress, such as harassment/bullying, have previously been discussed. Stress is a symptom, not an injury or even an occupational disease. However, again, a high incidence of stress-related disorders, perhaps as evidenced by absence, sickness and wastage rates, may indicate that the health and safety management of the workplace is inadequate. Some of the causes of stress, such as a workplace with poor security and lighting, may form the basis of an Improvement or Prohibition Notice or a prosecution by the safety inspectorate.

Appropriate responses by employers might involve the need to assess the impact of the work environment itself – premises, equipment and location as well as the organisation and management of work itself. It may be necessary to consider training to counteract stress, especially if the cause of the stress is hard to eliminate or minimise.

EXAMPLE – STRESS IN THE FIRE HEADQUARTERS

A report appeared on the incidence of stress-related disorders at the control centre of a large metropolitan fire service. It employed 82 staff on four 'watches' or shifts. All but three were women. The job was exacting in terms of responding quickly and effectively to emergencies. VDUs were introduced in 1979. Since then there had been complaints of birth defects in the women's children as well as a mounting incidence of headaches, depression, and a range of problems with the menstrual cycle. Staffing levels had dropped, causing additional stress and more resignations.

Safety inspectors examined some of the problems. Action could have been taken to enforce section 2 HSWA but was not at that time. (*Stress at Work* (1988) Labour Research Department)

It must also be remembered that in 1994 the first successful claim in negligence was made for stress at work.

THE SOCIAL WORKER: THE FIRST STRESS CASE

Mr Walker was a senior social worker. He had a difficult role and an increasing case load. He suffered a nervous breakdown and went on sick leave. When he returned, his case load had further increased and he was provided with no support or facilities to assist him. He suffered a second breakdown. He claimed in negligence that his employers had failed to take reasonable care of his health, especially bearing in mind that they could actually have predicted the harm in the light of his earlier breakdown. (*Walker v Northumberland CC*, 1994)

It is likely that claims for stress-related problems will grow. However, it should be noted that plaintiffs face considerable legal hurdles when developing their cases. In particular, they have to show:

- that the defendant (usually the employer) should have reasonably foreseen that if care was not taken at the workplace the plaintiff would have suffered stress;

- that reasonable care was not taken;

- that the lack of care was a cause of the stress, i.e. it was not all caused by other factors such as family bereavement, moving house or other well-documented stressful events.

## Workers with Disabilities

Many commentators are predicting that, with the likely impact of demographic changes in the 1990s, consequent skill shortages in some occupations and some areas will mean that employers will seek to recruit more people with disabilities who have been traditionally underemployed or unemployed. The legal system has traditionally provided little protection for such people, although the law of negligence has occasionally held that, because the consequences of an injury to people already with handicaps may be even more severe than for an able-bodied person, the employer should take proportionately greater care.

Health and safety legislation makes little specific reference to duties regarding employees with disabilities. However, MHSWR 1992 requires employers to become much better informed about factors which increase the vulnerability of particular employees. They will then have to make adequate provision by law. Obviously, disabilities regarding hearing, mobility and eyesight may demand changes to premises, but susceptibility to psychiatric disorders will also be covered.

The Disability Discrimination Act 1995 made some radical changes. It defines 'disability' in terms of significant impairment due to physical or psychological factors for the worker to perform day-to-day tasks. 'Significant' is an impairment which has lasted or is likely to last for one year or more.

It is unlawful to refuse to employ, promote or otherwise treat disadvantageously disabled persons and, more relevantly, the law requires health and safety adjustments to facilitate their working. Included here would be:

- adjustments to the building;
- provision of suitable equipment;
- changes to work stations;
- adaptability in working hours or working patterns;
- appropriate training;
- adjustment to in-house health and safety policies and procedures.

However, where the employer has fewer than 20 staff or where the costs of changes can be shown to be disproportionately expensive or complex, these rules do not apply. Case law is awaited on these points. In the meantime the prudent employer will explore ways of making the workplace and work avaiilable to people with disabilities and ensure that health and safety practices are given special attention.

In particular:

- Recruitment procedures must be fair towards disabled people; a disabled person should only be refused employment on health and safety grounds if the risks to which they will be exposed, or will create, will be material and substantial. Rather than supposition, evidence will have to be presented carefully to support the claim that this is a real risk.

- Workplaces should facilitate the needs of disabled people unless the costs of so doing are grossly disproportionate.

- Recruitment procedures should identify the nature and impact of an employee's disabilities for health and safety issues.

- Workplace practices should be sensitive to the needs of disabled people; managers need to be trained about disability issues and information about disabilities should only be disseminated using appropriate confidence levels.

- Psychological disability has to be treated in the same way as physical disability.

## HEALTH AND SAFETY AND NEW WORK PATTERNS

The 1980s and 1990s have seen dramatic growth in the number of self-employed, agency, temporary and part-time employees, and also in the use of subcontractors. More and more people are also working at home. Some of the issues surrounding these more varied, and often more autonomous, ways of working have already been touched on. However, there is a need to incorporate thinking on health and safety more generally in labour use strategies.

Many observers, not least the Health and Safety Executive itself, have noted the increased difficulty of maintaining good safety standards which this new and more fragmented workforce poses. In part, problems arise through physical/practical factors such as more complex lines of communication, different management systems and inconsistencies in approach. However, another factor is that health and safety legislation is built round the 'standard' employer/employee relationship and in some cases has little relevance to others, i.e. the self-employed. Some areas of law, for example negligence and occupiers' liability, are more wide ranging and flexible, but most are not. It is therefore necessary for employers of agency temps, subcontractors and those with employees at home to plan for and implement effective safety systems. As a minimum employers should do the following:

- Remember their duties to the self-employed – the need to provide them with safe premises and substances.

- Ensure before they use subcontractors, agencies or, indeed, the self-employed that adequate safety training and preparation are given to relevant employees in their own workforce.

- Provide for health and safety in every contract regarding such matters as:

  - insurance
  - indemnities
  - information on safety
  - safety and disciplinary procedures
  - provision for responding to breaches of safety standards.

- Ensure that individual employees are familiar with safety standards at the host workplace, know of safety policies and, ideally, have access to safety consultative procedures.

- Ensure adequate management and monitoring of the contract, with special reference to maintenance of health and safety standards.

- Monitor safety standards in order to identify any decline in standards which might be attributable to temps, subcontractors or greater use of self-employed persons; safety audits should encompass the impact of such contracts.

- If standards decline, develop adequate responses.

**Homeworkers**
Using homeworkers raises different health and safety issues, although much depends on whether or not they are employees. If they are employees, most of the normal provisions of HSWA, MHSWR and other regulations apply, regardless of where the work is performed. Of great

relevance are the regulations relating to display screens and hours of work. There have to be adequate inspections of equipment, work arrangements and employee health. It is clearly not a case of lowering safety standards.

Where homeworkers are self-employed much of the responsibility for safety passes to them. Employees moving to homeworking on a self-employed basis ought to be informed of the health and safety implications of the move.

## DEVELOPING HEALTH AND WELFARE POLICIES: SOME GENERAL ISSUES

Some of the emerging issues for law have led many employers to introduce formal policies which deal with smoking, alcohol and the like. They have generally evolved separately, although they frequently have much in common. Policies are often the product of professional advice and lengthy consultations with unions. Most will aim to provide information, advice and, in the case of smoking, drugs and alcohol, to provide support.

However, all such policies also have to deal with the situation of individuals breaking the 'rules' – continuing to get drunk, smoke or harass employees. It is important to appreciate the following when devising a strategy:

- Breaking the 'rules' of a policy should usually lead to some form of disciplinary action.

- Disciplinary action has to be contained in the contract of employment.

- Introducing a new 'offence' (of violence, smoking etc.) requires the contract to be amended accordingly.

- The amendment has to be carried out according to correct legal process; the new policy does not of itself do that, nor does a ballot of the workforce showing majority support for the policy.

- An effective change requires the agreement of individual employees which can be obtained in writing or, after the passage of a reasonable period of time, without objection.

- The new disciplinary procedure must adopt appropriate rules for the individual 'offences' and the procedures themselves must be fully and even-handedly applied in the event of an offence. The ACAS guidance *Discipline at Work* should be followed regarding investigations, interviews, evidence, hearings etc.

Policies and disciplinary procedures must stress the health and safety dimension. They must also, in order to be convincing in the event of action by the safety inspectorate or in law courts, be enforced, reviewed and, if necessary, amended. In addition to disciplinary procedures, such health and welfare policies will have to be incorporated in mainstream areas of personnel management. For example:

- Recruitment and selection – screening out smokers, drug abusers, those with violent or antisocial tendencies.

- Induction programmes – health and safety awareness.

- Contract documentation – disciplinary procedures, requirements for health checks, medical records etc.

- Occupational benefits – assistance for smokers/addicts etc., welfare benefits, counselling facilities.

- Career management – management and training should be linked with effective policy development and implementation.

## CONCLUSIONS AND STRATEGIES

The law is changing in both content and emphasis. Safety management is now seen as the area of greatest interest and the avenue through which improvements will be made. Safety issues have to percolate through organisational decision making at all levels. For example, they ought to play an integral part in the following central decisions, as well as in the more ongoing facets of management:

- relocation of workplace;

- refurbishing of premises;

- development of new labour-use strategies – use of agencies, subcontractors etc.;

- purchase of all workplace equipment;

- review of managerial responsibilities.

# Index